LOVED *and* PROTECTED

Joy & Blessings,
Asha

LOVED *and* PROTECTED

Stories of Miracles and Answered Prayers

ASHA PRAVER

Crystal Clarity Publishers, Nevada City, CA 95959
Copyright © 2013 Hansa Trust
All rights reserved. Published 2013

Printed in China.

ISBN 13: 978-1-56589-275-0
ePub ISBN: 978-1-56589-523-2

Cover design and interior design and layout by Tejindra Scott Tully

Library of Congress Cataloging-in-Publication Data

Praver, Asha.
  Loved and protected : stories of miracles and answered prayers / Asha
       Praver. -- 1st [edition].
     pages cm
  ISBN 978-1-56589-275-0 (quality pbk. : alk. paper) -- ISBN 978-
       1-56589-523-2 (epub)
1. Spiritual life. 2. Miracles. 3. Prayer. I. Title.

 BP605.S4P73 2013
 248.4--dc23
                        2013013347

www.crystalclarity.com / 800.424.1055 – 530.478.7600

Dedicated to Everyone

*"If you knew how much God loves you,
you would die for joy."*

~ St. Jean Vianney ~

Contents

PART ONE: *God's Hand*

Sudden Change | 15

Free Fall | 17

Divine Currents | 19

Master's Message | 21

Church of Starbucks | 23

Prayers of a Devout Mother | 24

Fumes in the Night | 28

Godspeed | 30

Wheee! | 32

God Changes His Mind | 33

Collision Course | 35

Even a Sparrow | 36

A Higher Law | 38

Fire Ceremony | 40

Driving Lesson | 42

Minus One | 44

First Day of Vacation | 46

Seek and Ye Shall Find | 48

Friends in High Places | 51

Lane Change | 53

Hand in Hand | 55

On the Way to Italy | 59

AUM | 62

PART TWO: *Unexpected Gifts*

God Remembers | 67

Shower of Blessings | 69

No?! | 71

Happy Ending | 73

My Invisible Friend | 76

Long Walk Home | 78

Roar of the Lion | 81

Motherhood | 84

No Introduction Needed | 86

Friends to the End | 88

Make Rich the Soil | 92

Why Me? | 94

Conscious Conception | 97

Arranged Marriage | 98

Shoes On, Shoes Off | 100

He Knows Your Need | 103

No More Tears | 106

Emergency Care | 107

New Flight Plan | 109

Doctor Shanti | 111

It Is All Arranged | 114

Travel Plans | 116

Rose Song | 118

Actions Speak Louder than Words | 121

PART THREE: *Follow Me*

Long Way Around | 125

Twice Blessed | 129

Recommended Reading | 131

Marching Orders | 132

New Wine | 134

Homeward Bound | 136

Believe | 138

PART FOUR: *Problem Solved*

Two-Up | 143

Check! | 146

Falling Rain | 148

Home Sweet Home | 150

And the Answer Is . . . | 152

A Good Question | 154

Fear No More | 156

Divine Efficiency | 159

Good Car-ma | 161

The Ten-Percent Solution | 163

Right Time, Right Prayer | 165

She Knows | 167

Perfect Timing | 170

Better to Know | 171

Homecoming | 173

House Plans | 176

Above the Clouds | 178

Go Green | 181

You Have Mail | 183

Go! | 185

GR8 | 187

Highway Patrol | 189

Happily Ever After | 191

Mother's Care | 194

The Right Foundation | 196

Time | 199

Stonewalled | 201

In Case of Fire | 203

PART FIVE: *Healing Presence*

Breathe Easy | 209
Good Medicine | 211
Divine Therapy | 212
The Comforter | 214
Kitty Bliss | 215
Puzzled | 217
Angel Wings | 219
I Sing Your Song | 221
Gone | 224
Never Too Late | 225
Hard Lesson | 228
Hands Across the Sea | 231
One Life Beneath the Surface | 233
Nor for Myself, Lord | 237
Dear Cancer Cells . . . | 239

Saved | 261
Valentine | 262
Vehicle for the Divine | 263
Right Number | 266
Rescued | 268
Rainfall and Moonlight | 269
My Child | 271
Peace at Last | 273
Across the Water | 275
Our Lady | 278
Let There Be Light | 280
White Bird | 283
Desert Hike | 286
Two Nurses | 290
Rock in the Snow Field | 292

PART SIX: *God Comes*

Grandpa and the Lady | 245
Picture Perfect | 247
Am I Not Always with You? | 249
A Dark and Stormy Night | 251
Hansa | 253
NOW! | 256
More Than a Lifetime | 258

INTRODUCTION

This book is for those who want a deeper, more trusting relationship with God, and who find inspiration and hope in the experiences of others who seek also to know Him.

Some of the stories told here are quite dramatic. In a split second, the fabric of the universe rearranges itself and inevitable catastrophe is averted by forces more subtle than the senses can perceive.

Other experiences of God come quietly, in answer to everyday concerns like buying a home, caring for aging relatives, finding a mate, or fixing a car.

Before I wrote this book, if you had asked me, "Do you believe in the power of prayer?" without hesitation, I would have said, "Yes." I have lived in spiritual community for more than forty years and the evidence is all around me.

Still, I was not prepared for what I saw in the eyes of those who shared their stories with me. How tenderly, how sensitively, how *personally* God responds. Not just to the prominent or talented, the rich or articulate, but to *everyone* who sincerely calls to Him.

"God feels for us," Paramhansa Yogananda wrote in his *Autobiography of a Yogi*. "He is not partial to a few, but listens to everyone who approaches Him trustingly. His children should ever have implicit faith in the loving-kindness of their Omnipresent Father."

Prayer is not a ritual to be carried out in a formal way at specified times. Prayer is a conversation, an ongoing heart-to-Heart. Every day we talk to friends and relatives, to coworkers, store clerks, and hairdressers about our hopes and disappointments, our losses and needs.

Why not talk also to the One who has the answers?

Many contributors to this book follow the path of Self-realization. Their stories include references to aspects of that path, which are mostly explained in context, as well as references to certain persons. Babaji, a deathless Himalayan yogi, is one in the Self-realization line of gurus. Paramhansa Yogananda, author of *Autobiography of a Yogi*, is the most recent guru and best known. His devotees call him "Master." Sri Yukteswar was the guru of Yogananda. And Swami Kriyananda, "Swamiji," is the founder of Ananda, a global network of spiritual communities.

GOD'S HAND

*"Though man's ingenuity for getting himself
into trouble appears to be endless,
the Infinite Succor is no less resourceful."*

LAHIRI MAHASAYA
~ Autobiography of a Yogi ~

SUDDEN CHANGE

In winter, there is a "magic line" on Highway I-90 in Washington state where the rain stops and the snow begins. Many accidents happen when drivers meet this sudden change in the weather. To make it even worse, the "magic line" is preceded by a long blind curve. I'm a firefighter, part of a first-response medical team. I know that stretch of highway all too well.

This was a typical call. On a cold November morning, a vehicle had spun out and rolled over at that spot. Fortunately, the driver was only moderately hurt. We got him out of the car, strapped him to a backboard, and loaded him into the medical vehicle. I was the crew chief and it was my job to ensure the safety of the whole scene.

Cars were still coming fast around the blind curve, unaware of the accident scene and the treacherous conditions. I began walking toward the curve, facing traffic, placing flares in the middle of the road to warn drivers of what was ahead. My partner Glen, working in the medical vehicle, kept watch on me out the back window.

As I placed the last flare I saw a car, coming too fast around the curve, lose control and go into a spin. He was headed right for me.

Suddenly, I was no longer standing in the middle of the road, but fifty feet away on the shoulder. I don't know how I got there. It happened in an instant. The car hurtled right through the spot where I'd been standing, then swerved down the road, sideswiped our medical vehicle, careened off another car, and slid into a ditch.

The car was wrecked, but the driver was okay. My crew emerged from the medical vehicle with only minor bumps and scratches.

My partner, Glen, rushed over to me, grabbed my shoulders and yelled into my face, "Are you okay?!"

He had watched the whole scene. One moment I'd been in the path of death, and the next moment I was gone. He was sure I'd been killed.

I couldn't explain it either. We walked together to that spot in the road.

We saw my footprints and the tire marks where the car should have hit me, and my footprints fifty feet away on the shoulder.

There were no footprints in between.

—from Brian Dotson

FREE FALL

I don't know who saw the bird first, but all four of us rose from our seats and headed to the window to see it more clearly. I was visiting the home of Parvati and Pranaba for the first time, and it never occurred to me that an open stairwell leading to the basement was on the other side of the half-wall to my right.

I was behind the others and couldn't see the bird, so I took a step backward and to the side hoping to get a better view. Instead of solid floor, however, my foot went into space. I was close enough to grab my wife's shoulder to break my fall, but consciously chose not to, for fear of pulling her with me to wherever I was going.

I was pretty reckless in my youth, falling off of every moving thing a boy can ride on—bike, skateboard, surfboard, snowboard—you name it, I've fallen off of it. Fortunately, I always escaped without serious injury.

So when I found myself horizontal in the air going backwards, it was a space I had been in before. I rotated my body to face into the fall and saw that I was going head first down a long, steep stairwell. "This is going to be a hard fall," I thought. "Maybe this time I won't get away unscathed."

Then I heard a voice of power like I have never heard before. "Oh! God! NO!" It was Parvati. Usually such an exclamation at such a moment would be tinged with fear, pleading, or regret.

Not this time.

This was a commandment to the Universe, and the Universe complied.

Without any transition or time passing, I found myself standing right where I had intended to go when my foot went into the stairwell—behind my wife, looking out the window. It was as if what had happened just previous to that had been only a dream. Both my feet were now firmly on the floor with the stairwell behind my heels.

Later, when we compared notes, all of us had seen the same thing. I was falling down the staircase. Parvati exclaimed. Then I was standing looking out the window.

Pranaba told us that the night before he had dreamt that *he* fell down the staircase. Was he dreaming my karma? Did I take his? Or did Parvati, as an instrument of Divine Will, avert a terrible accident for both of us?

—from Turiya

DIVINE CURRENTS

I vaguely remember that there was a sign, saying: "Dangerous Currents. No Lifeguard." I grew up in the middle of the United States. At age twenty I had hardly ever seen an ocean and certainly knew very little about them, so the sign meant nothing to me. It was a beautiful sunny day, and there I was in California at the Pacific Ocean. All I could think about was diving into those waves.

Paddling around in the water, I reveled in this new experience. Then everything changed. I was caught in a rip tide and it was carrying me away from shore. I fought against it, but the current was too strong. Farther and farther it took me out into the sea, until the crashing surf was tossing me about like a rag doll.

I struggled and struggled to no avail. I was fighting for my life and the ocean was winning. Finally, unable to swim another stroke, I turned over onto my back and literally went "belly up." I was convinced there was nothing I could do and no one who could save me.

Waves were crashing around me, but I felt completely calm. I had never considered what I would do when faced with death. In hindsight,

I am surprised by my response. I had just started meditating recently, and I knew God was out there somewhere. I wasn't sure, though, what role He might play in my life, and what my relationship was to Him.

Now, as I looked at the vast blue sky, the bright sun, and the ocean around me, I offered myself completely to God. No words. I wasn't asking to be saved. I didn't pray to die quickly. With all my heart, I just gave myself back to Him.

What happened next seemed the most natural thing in the world. In response to my self-offering, God gave me bliss. Self-offering equals bliss: It is a lesson I have never forgotten.

Basking in His bliss, it took me a few minutes to realize that I was now floating in calm water. I rested there until my strength returned. Then I dog-paddled in a channel of calm water all the way back to shore.

—from Devarshi

MASTER'S MESSAGE

When I found out I had breast cancer, everyone told me, "Have surgery as soon as possible." I was not so much in a hurry. First I wanted to understand from Master why he had sent this to me and how—perhaps even *if*—he wanted me to be healed.

When I heard, though, soon after I was diagnosed, about one of the most famous and skilled physicians in Italy, who specialized in breast cancer, I decided to go forward and see if this was what Master wanted.

My husband and I called and were able to get an appointment with the doctor for the next day. When I arrived at his office, something felt dissonant. I couldn't explain it. He had the best reputation, but he didn't feel like the right one for me.

I explained to my husband my perplexing feeling, but he wanted to go ahead with the pre-surgery exams anyway. When it was all done, we arranged to see the doctor again when all the paperwork was in. In Italy we have a national medical system, and everything has to be documented in advance.

When all the papers were ready, I went for my next scheduled visit.

To my astonishment the doctor refused to see me! He said he was too busy and I would have to come back another time.

Very strongly I felt, "This is not the doctor to operate on me."

I told my husband, but because he was so worried about me, and this doctor was supposed to be the best in Italy, he tried to persuade me to go ahead. Something stronger than I made me refuse even my husband.

In meditation that night, I said to Master, "I want your will, not mine. I need to understand clearly. Please write for me what you want me to do." After that, I went peacefully to sleep.

In the morning we went to the community temple for yoga and meditation. When we came home we saw that someone had slipped a handwritten note under the door.

I said to my husband, "This is a note from Master." My certainty surprised my spouse. I had not told him about my prayer.

The note was from my friend Laura telling me about another doctor in a nearby town who also specialized in the care I needed. He was not famous or rich, but Laura felt I should try him.

When my husband and I went to see this doctor, we knew immediately he was just the right one. He performed the operation and everything went perfectly.

Seven months later we heard that at the very time that famous doctor would have operated on me, if I had let him, two other women had surgery by him. Both had serious troubles afterwards. One will be affected for the rest of her life. That doctor is now under investigation.

—from Vinaya

CHURCH *of* STARBUCKS

We were speeding down the freeway in the far left lane, heading back to Los Angeles after a week at Ananda Village. My husband, Vasanta, was driving; two friends were in the back seat. We were about ten minutes away from our agreed-upon breakfast stop.

Suddenly, without forethought, I said, "Let's stop for coffee!" Vasanta is a coffee gourmet and had made converts of us, so the immediate "Yes!" from all present was no surprise.

Still, I had barely finished my sentence before Vasanta crossed three lanes of traffic and started down the exit ramp. The moment we were safely off the freeway, the transmission seized up, stalling the engine and cutting off power to the brakes and steering. Fortunately, there was no traffic, and the car coasted safely to a stop—right in front of Starbucks!

If Vasanta had hesitated at all, we would still have been on the freeway when he lost control of the car.

I don't think any church uses coffee *during* the communion service, but for us it will always be a holy beverage!

—*from Maghi*

PRAYERS *of a*
DEVOUT MOTHER

I was a compliant child and joined without question the daily prayers and three-times-a-week church services that defined our family life. My grandparents had been missionaries to India. My father was the music minister and my mother a devoted member of the evangelical, born-again Christian church we all attended.

I wasn't just being obedient. As a child, I had my own sweet connection with Jesus.

By the time I went to college, though, none of it made sense to me anymore. I had to throw away that whole worldview, including the Bible. I didn't, however, leave God entirely. Or perhaps it would be more accurate to say, He didn't leave me. When I stopped going to church, He started meeting me out in Nature. Sometimes, hiking through the mountains, the beauty I saw moved me so deeply that, overcome with feelings of joy and love, I wept tears of gratitude.

Still, the "God" I had known as a child I held at a distance. Enough of surrendering my will to His! Ego was in charge of my life now.

Three classmates and I were commuting one day from our morning lab to our afternoon seminar at the University of Washington Medical Center. The woman driving had borrowed her boyfriend's car: a Renault Dauphine that he was very proud of and had spent a lot of money fixing up.

Even though we had plenty of time for the commute, she was excited to be driving his car. When we got on the freeway, she accelerated to seventy-five miles per hour, twenty miles more than the speed limit. From the backseat I could see she wasn't a very experienced driver and was completely unfamiliar with this rear-engine car.

A big Cadillac to the right of us, going about fifty-five, moved into our lane. The driver had no idea how fast we were going and miscalculated the distance. Seeing us rushing toward a collision with the Cadillac's rear end, my friend instinctively hit the brakes and simultaneously turned the wheel, trying to swerve around the Cadillac. The weight of the rear engine began to bring the back end forward, turning the car sideways to the road. My friend, in pure primal instinct now, overcorrected, and we fishtailed back and forth across three lanes of freeway traffic before crashing into a twenty-foot concrete wall.

The fishtailing had slowed us down, but we were still going about forty-five miles an hour when we hit. This was in the days before seatbelts were required, so none of us were wearing one.

The front of the car made first contact with the wall, at a forty-five-degree angle. The car then bounced off the wall and did a complete sideways somersault, landing solidly on all four tires. The impact shattered the glass in every window. The rear suspension buckled. One side of the roof and the whole front of the car were demolished.

Inside the car, we sat for a few seconds in stunned silence. The most generous-hearted of my friends was the first to speak. "Are you all right?

Are you all right?" she asked. True to her nature, her concern was for everyone else.

The driver, seeing what a wreck she had made of the vehicle, began wailing and crying, "Oh, my God! Oh, my God! My boyfriend is going to kill me! He just put seven hundred dollars into this car!" (That was a lot of money in 1970 when this happened.)

The whole thing could not have been more perfectly engineered to destroy the car but save our lives. We did not sustain a single injury. Not a bruise. Not a scratch.

Trembling with nerves, we sorted through a million little pieces of glass to gather up our strewn books and bags. A Washington State Patrol car took us the rest of the way to our destination, and a few minutes later we were sitting in our college classroom waiting for the lecture to begin.

Three days afterward I was commuting by bicycle from my dorm to the lab. When I left home, it was clear and sunny. By the time I started back in the late afternoon, a hard rain was falling. The ride home included a long, straight, downhill section, but a little rain couldn't dampen my enthusiasm for what was definitely the most fun part. Down the hill I pedaled as fast as I could on my narrow-rim tires, accelerating to thirty-five or forty miles per hour as I raced toward the place where the street leveled off. There were two lanes going each way, and I was actually passing cars moving more slowly than I was because of the wet conditions.

At the bottom of the hill, a small side street came in from the right. I saw a car waiting at the stop sign there. Then he pulled into my two lanes, intending to cross them and turn left uphill on the other side of the road. I calculated how long it would take him to get across my lanes. I compared it to the speed I was moving, heading directly toward him.

"No problem," I thought. "I don't even have to slow down. As he goes forward, I'll just scoot around behind him on the far right." This was fortunate, because with wet tires, wet brakes, and wet pavement, it wouldn't be easy for me to stop.

Suddenly I saw something I had not noticed before in the fading light with all the rain. There was traffic coming up the hill in the two left lanes where the driver intended to turn. He saw it at the same time I did.

Instead of turning left, as I had counted on him doing, he shifted into reverse and started backing toward the side street again. He started going backwards just as I started to arc around behind him. Except now there was no "behind him"—just the full length of his car right where I was heading.

With all my strength I squeezed both my handbrakes. The wheels locked and the bike went perpendicular to the road, facing the side street. Sliding sideways, I was tipped over so far my handlebar almost touched the street.

"I'm going right under that car," I thought, "and I'm not going to survive."

Suddenly time, space, thought, and vision ceased to exist. I felt a force move my body and my bicycle in a smooth, seemingly effortless motion—not sideways into the car, but forward over the curb and onto the sidewalk, out of harm's way. When thought and vision returned, I was there on my bike, facing toward home.

Twice in four days death had come racing toward me, but Something had held it at bay. What was going on here?

"How fragile and precious life is," I thought. "Guardian angels must be real."

I wrote to my parents, sparing them the details, but humbly inquiring, "Have you been praying for me?"

"Yes, of course," they replied. "We pray for you every day."

—from Jagadeesh

FUMES *in the* NIGHT

Alcoholism and substance abuse were our family business—the one thing we all did well. No one even noticed when, as a child, I helped clean up after my parents' bridge parties by drinking the last drops of liquor left in the bottom of each glass.

I started drinking on my own when I was thirteen. By sixteen I was pretty regular, and by eighteen I was a full-blown alcoholic. At nineteen I married an alcoholic; and at twenty-five I got divorced, but didn't stop drinking. I functioned fine on the outside. I would work during the day and drink during the night. That's the way we did it in my family.

Eventually I got married again. My husband had no clue what was going on. I'd have a few drinks with him over dinner and go to bed more or less when he did. In the middle of the night, when he was sound asleep, I would get up and spend several hours drinking alone. I had become my mother.

Even though no one was trying to stop me—no one even knew what I was doing—sometimes I would obsess for six hours a day about how and when I would get my next drink. My mind was always on it.

Things went on this way for many years. Odd as it may seem, I was a successful businesswoman and a fitness instructor. I began to meditate, and I regularly led group meditation and healing sessions. I knew I was lacking integrity in presenting myself as a leader that way, but I was powerless to stop.

Early one morning I awoke to an all-pervasive smell of alcohol in the bedroom. One of my most vivid childhood memories is opening the door of my parents' room early in the morning and being assaulted by a wave of alcohol fumes. My mother, having gone to bed after hours of drinking, had been breathing into the closed room all night.

She had died years earlier—of alcoholism, of course—and I thought her spirit had come to visit me. As part of my healing work I channeled spirits from the other side, so it seemed natural that she might come.

"Mother," I said, "is that you?"

Then, in a sickening wave of grief, I realized that the smell of alcohol was not coming from my mother; it was coming from me. I got out of bed, went into the dark living room, and fell on my knees and prayed.

"Lord," I said, "you *must* help me. *I can't go on living this way.*"

This time God must have known I was serious, because I never drank again. Not that it was easy. Adult Children of Alcoholics, Alcoholics Anonymous, Twelve Steps—I worked my programs with every ounce of strength I had and all the strength God gave me.

Even now, twenty-one years later, I never take my sobriety for granted. To me it will always be a miracle from God.

—from Anonymous

GODSPEED

In East Texas, folks have a lot of room in which to spread out. It is a long way from here to there, no matter where you start or where you are going. On the country roads, especially late at night, you drive fast, without much regard for speed limits.

I was pretty new on the meditation path and thrilled to discover that one of my customers in Tyler, Texas, was also a meditator. I made him the last stop of the day so we could meet afterwards for dinner and meditation. My hotel was an hour away in Longview. I had to be ready bright and early the next day, but I often traveled to that area from my home base in Dallas. So I felt comfortable with the drive.

We had a lovely dinner, a peaceful walk in the country, and a great meditation. It was pretty late when I started toward Longview. I was making good time down the dark, deserted road, feeling warmly connected to God and Guru, when I heard a voice say, "Slow down!" I was startled and lifted my foot a little off the gas pedal. Soon the same voice spoke again, more forcefully. "*Slow down!*" This time I hit the brake, and brought my speed down to twenty-five miles an hour.

A minute later, I rounded a blind curve and found myself heading straight into a small herd of cattle ambling across the road. Cows are big, heavy creatures. A head-on collision can demolish a car and severely injure, even kill, the driver.

I was seconds away from crashing into the broad side of a cow when an Unseen Hand took over and steered me safely through the herd. My hands remained on the wheel, but I was just along for the ride.

Seconds later, back on the open road, I was in charge again. If I had been going faster than twenty-five miles an hour, I don't think even an Unseen Hand could have saved me from a serious accident.

—from Katy Radha Rice

WHEEE!

My head and arms were hanging out the car window, the way a dog likes to ride with his snout into the wind. I was about five years old in the era before children were strapped into car seats. My father's best friend, "Uncle Mac," was driving. Dad was sitting next to him.

It was a curvy road and every time we went around a bend, I squealed with delight.

At a certain point a voice said to me, "Go see what your father and Uncle Mac are doing." Although I couldn't remember when I had heard it before, the voice was familiar to me, and it didn't seem odd that it was speaking now.

"Okay," I said, pulling my head in and flopping my arms over the center back of the front seat.

In that instant, the door I had been leaning against swung wide open.

Uncle Mac immediately pulled over. In stunned silence we contemplated how close we had come to tragedy.

—from Richard

GOD CHANGES HIS MIND

Full-immersion baptism is not an Ananda practice. Three days after I came to the temple for the first time, God decided to try it on me anyway to see if it might do some good.

I was repairing the tin roof of a houseboat moored on the Willamette River, a quarter of a mile above the falls. The roof was steep and slick, and I wasn't dressed right for the job. I needed flexible shoes with good traction. Instead, I was up there in my heavy construction boots.

It was spring and the river was running hard, fast, and high, with a strong undertow pulling toward the falls. Just two weeks earlier, one of the houseboats had been ripped from its moorings and was barely saved from going down those falls.

I remember being on the roof, leaning over to nail down the next piece of tin sheeting. Then I was stretched full out in the air, about to do a massive belly flop into the river in the four feet of space between the rafts to which the houseboats are lashed. Even that four feet was crowded with pillars and guy wires.

Turned out it didn't matter, because I never did that belly flop. The next thing that happened was me pulling myself up onto the raft of the neighboring houseboat—with no bruises, cuts, or broken bones. To make it even more odd, I had been going down belly first, but as I came out of the water I noticed that the sides and front of my upper body were dry, except for where I had brushed against the raft as I climbed out.

I'm a big man: 6'3", 220 pounds. The roof I fell from was at least fifteen feet above the river. I was wearing a fully loaded tool belt and, as I mentioned, my heavy construction boots, plus a wool jacket. All my tools, the cell phone from my pocket, and the glasses from my face were sucked into the water. But my chest didn't even get wet.

I guess God decided that, at least for me, full-immersion baptism wasn't needed after all.

—from Peter Copley

COLLISION COURSE

The back roads were so much prettier than Highway 6. So even though it took longer, that was my route back and forth to work. It was starting to snow, and as I made the turn off the highway, an inner voice said, "Stay on Route 6." But I ignored it. Later there was another chance to return to the highway; but when the inner voice again urged me to take that route, I said out loud, "No."

Not long after, going downhill, I began to slide on the now-icy road. Another driver, waiting at a stop sign, saw me coming, but pulled into the intersection anyway. I plowed into her car, pushing it into a ditch. Fortunately, no one was hurt.

When my car stopped I spoke out loud. "I will *never* not listen to You again."

Some years later I was driving home from work in the left lane of an expressway. My exit was coming up and I needed to think about getting over to the right. Suddenly an urgent inner message came: "Move over now!"

This time I didn't hesitate but immediately changed lanes. Within seconds, a fast-moving vehicle hit from behind the car in the spot I had just vacated.

—from Dhiren

EVEN *a* SPARROW

The village in India where my parents live is surrounded by hills and is accessible only by car. The nearest train station is seventy kilometers away. I was going to school in America. As soon as vacation started I took a plane to New Delhi, then a train as close as it would take me. My father met me in his small car and we began the drive home.

The road twisted and turned with a steep hill on one side and a steep valley on the other. About ten kilometers from our village, in the middle of a sharp turn, suddenly the engine stopped completely and the steering froze. Instead of completing the turn we kept going forward, heading right for the steep drop-off into the valley below.

My father and I were too shocked to speak. We looked silently at one another, our eyes wide with fear.

I was so frightened I couldn't even pray. I closed my eyes and waited for the car to topple down the hill. A single thought came, "Dear God, how can this be happening? I haven't even seen my mother yet."

At that moment the car came to a sudden stop. The nose had run into a small mound of soil at the very edge of the road, put there perhaps to stop erosion. The car was battered by the impact. We were shaken up. I had a cut on my knee, but otherwise we were unscathed.

Bad karma had been mitigated. Why? We didn't know.

A few days later we revisited the place where the near-accident had happened. My father remembered that shortly before he went to pick me up, he had stopped at exactly that same spot. A little bird had fallen onto the road. Concerned that it might be run over by a car, he had stopped, picked up the bird, and moved it safely into the trees nearby.

—from Vidya

A HIGHER LAW

Getting a visa to visit the United States from my home country is no easy matter. Our government doesn't want to lose any more citizens to that land of much greater opportunity. And the U.S. isn't exactly recruiting new residents from where I was born. Several people I knew, including a member of my family, had already tried and failed.

Still, when I heard about the Yoga Teacher Training course offered at Ananda Village in California, I decided I had to come. I am trained as a lawyer, so I went about preparing the documents in my most lawyerly way. I started with a formal letter of invitation from Ananda that explained what the course was about and how long it would last, to show that my intention was to go to the U.S. and then return home.

I even prepared a speech and rehearsed it word for word in my mind.

Finally the big day came, and there I was standing in front of the consul. Suddenly my mind went absolutely blank. I managed to hand him the letter of invitation but forgot all the other documents, even though they were right there in my purse. Every word of my prepared speech disappeared from memory.

Without any conscious decision on my part, I found myself mentally chanting, "God, I love You. God, I love You. God, I love You." I was behaving as if I were in front of my meditation altar in the privacy of my home, not standing before the consul trying to get a visa. But I was unable to do anything except silently repeat, "God, I love You."

The consul carefully examined the letter of invitation. "How nice that you are going to train as a yoga teacher," he said with a warm smile. "Yoga is a very useful discipline."

Even when, a few minutes later, he handed me my multiple entry visa into the United States, my mind stayed blank except for "God, I love You."

Friends and family were amazed that I got the visa at all, and incredulous when they heard that it was given to me without benefit of any of my carefully prepared materials.

My only explanation was, "Seek ye first the kingdom of God, and all these things shall be added unto you."

—from Anonymous

FIRE CEREMONY

If you live in the woods, you soon get to know the engine sound of a borate bomber: the small plane that drops fire retardant chemicals on wildfires. So when I heard that sound, I looked out the window for signs of fire. I was in the Ananda Meditation Retreat kitchen fixing dinner for staff and guests. I saw neither smoke nor flames, so I figured it wasn't nearby.

At the same moment, a staff person was saying to a guest, "No, I don't think it's a bomber. If it were we'd see . . ."

His conversation was abruptly terminated when the plane dropped its full load of borate into a densely wooded area about two hundred yards away.

Just then, another staff person raced into the kitchen, grabbed the phone and called the fire department. When he heard the engine noise, he had climbed a tree and from that vantage point saw what we couldn't: a cabin near the kitchen, surrounded by tall trees, was on fire.

We rushed over and saw the cabin already engulfed in flames. Fortunately, there was no wind, so the fire went straight up, and the borate all around kept it from spreading. A minute later, the volunteer fire department arrived and doused the flames. We are way out in the woods and usually it takes much longer for them to reach us.

Later, we pieced together the sequence of events. It was a miracle of God's perfect timing.

First, a child on a bicycle rode past and saw no sign of fire. Ten minutes later the cabin burst into flames; we still don't know why. At that very moment, a borate bomber on its way to another fire saw the cabin burning and got permission to drop its load there. The call from the plane was also picked up by the local volunteer fire department. They were on their way to put out the fire before we even knew there was one.

The couple that lived in the cabin were not home, so nothing was saved. Everything was reduced to ashes. When the ashes cooled, we started cleaning up the site. On a nearby bush, we found an eloquent reminder of Who is really in charge of our lives.

One page from *Autobiography of a Yogi* had survived. Neatly charred around the edges, the face untouched, it was the frontispiece photo of Master.

—*from Anandi*

DRIVING LESSON

It was 5:00 p.m., already dark and snowing hard. Only those who had to be there were out on the road. At age twenty-six, that included me. I had a date with my girlfriend and no mere blizzard was going to keep me from her. I know how to drive in snow.

There were two lanes in each direction. The plows had been through and the center divide was piled high with snow. In the far right lane, going my direction, commuters were making their cautious way home at a steady twenty-five miles per hour.

I had the left lane all to myself and was going thirty-five to forty. I was halfway past a group of about ten cars, when suddenly one of the commuters pulled into my lane. Either he was blinded by the conditions or he hadn't even looked back, never imagining someone would be coming up so fast on his left.

I was going so much faster than the car in front of me that just taking my foot off the accelerator wouldn't slow me enough. But if I hit the brakes, I would skid into the cars next to me, or slam into the snow piled on the other side. A collision was inevitable.

That's when I blacked out.

The next thing I knew I was in the right-hand lane in *front* of the whole line of cars I had been passing. My car was fishtailing like crazy and my only thought was, "I have to get control of the car." Which I did; I know how to drive in snow.

What happened to the guy who had pulled in front of me? I'll never know.

I was not a religious person at that time. So my first, second, and third thoughts were not "Thank you, God." But I knew Someone had taken over the driving and put me back in the car only when He knew I could handle it.

Although it took years for the seed to sprout, this was the beginning of my spiritual awakening. From then on I knew that this world is not what it seems.

—from Uddhava

Minus One

Hiking into our remote campsite, I named the steep mile of loose shale "the Slippery Slide." I said my mantra, *AUM Guru*, with double intensity, and we made it safely up; but I wasn't looking forward to the return trip down.

After a few blissful days in the high country—no other people, no cell phones—it was time to go. When we got to the Slippery Slide, I walked in front of my wife so I could catch her if she fell. "If you start to lose your balance," I told her, "fall *up*hill."

"AUM Guru, AUM Guru, AUM Guru," I repeated inwardly as we made our way down. I was carrying the majority of the load, about sixty-five pounds in a high-frame backpack that extended above my head and strapped across my upper chest. I always wear my *rudraksha mala* (meditation prayer beads) inside my shirt against my skin. The strap, however, pressed uncomfortably against the hard beads, so when backpacking I wore it on top.

About halfway down the Slide I looked back to see how my wife was doing. That slight turn was enough to shift my center of gravity. Suddenly, I was airborne. A branch flashed by and I tried to grab it, but the hiking pole strapped to my wrist got in the way. I wasn't at all afraid, just interested in what might happen next.

Gravity brought me down pack-first, cushioning my spine and head from the worst of the impact. I lay there stunned with my feet pointing uphill, my head pointing down, staring at the sky. After a moment I undid the strap, rolled off the pack and stood up. I was quite calm. My wife, however, was a different story. She'd watched the whole thing, which apparently looked worse to her than it felt to me.

It didn't help that, like in some corny horror movie, blood was pouring down my arm and dripping from my fingertips. I thought it looked cool, but understandably, my wife freaked out. I had a puncture wound in my forearm, probably from the mid-air grab at the branch. During the eight-mile walk back to the car, the bandage soaked through twice. We made it home safely though, and the doctor confirmed that nothing was seriously wrong.

A few days later I was in the middle of my Thursday morning, long meditation where I always do 108 kriyas, one full circle of my *mala*. Somewhere around kriya number ninety, I felt something odd. Where there should have been a bead, there was an empty section of wire. *Rudraksha* beads are hard and small, the seed of a tree in India. It must have taken a direct hit to break the bead, leave the wire intact, and not break my rib in the process.

This was clearly a case of what I call "mitigated karma." My destiny demanded that an accident happen. The protection of God and Guru, however, turned what could have been tragic into a mere (though bloody) inconvenience. Life and limb were spared, but the karmic energy had to go *somewhere*.

As a cosmic joke (or so it seems to me), in exchange for my life, God took one *rudraksha* bead.

—*from Vasanta*

First Day
of Vacation

It was late afternoon before we were packed and ready to leave on our vacation. My husband had been up all night; I'd slept only a few hours. We thought about waiting until the next morning, but decided against it.

My husband was driving and I was in the passenger seat when apparently we both fell sound asleep. The next thing we knew, we were crashing down a steep embankment heading for a ditch. He woke up just in time to slam on the brakes with such force that the torpedo-shaped roof box, true to its name, kept on going even when the car itself came to a jolting halt.

A truck driver saw us go over the edge and was on the spot in a matter of seconds. Fortunately, we weren't hurt; nor was the car. Even the "torpedo" was fine. It was a steep drive back up to the road, but we made it.

Looking back over the edge, for the first time we noticed a line of big poles running parallel to the ditch about the width of a parking space apart. Easy for a careful driver to avoid; a lethal hazard for someone asleep at the wheel. The poles stood evenly spaced in both directions as far as we could see—except for one wide gap right where our car had plunged through.

—from Mantradevi

Seek *and* Ye Shall Find

don't know what possessed me to buy a motorcycle. Maybe it was the fact that I was nineteen and didn't know what else to do with myself. I rode the motorbike, but never felt confident on it, especially on the freeway.

On the Fourth of July 1975, I set out with a couple of friends on a motorcycle trip to somewhere. They were together on one bike; I was riding alone. We took off down the freeway, and soon we were going much faster than I had ever gone before. They were riding ahead of me and I had to keep up.

There was a dip in the road, and a sharp turn with a sign: "Speed Limit 55 MPH." I was going way over that. The speedometer was pushing eighty. My handlebars started to shake. I didn't have the skill to deal with what was happening.

I wasn't wearing a helmet or any special gear, just jeans and a light jacket. I remember sliding backwards off the motorcycle, going very fast as if I had been shot out of a cannon. The next thing I knew I was standing in the middle of the freeway, watching the traffic whiz around me. The bike was a little distance away, lying sideways on the road.

My friends saw what had happened and circled back to get me. I was stunned and had some pretty nasty road burns, but otherwise I was unhurt. No concussion or internal injuries, and no broken bones.

I wouldn't get back on that bike, though, not for anything in the world. I never really rode it again after that. It started up fine, and my friend rode it home. A truck driver who stopped to help gave me a ride.

Back then I had barely started to make my way in life, and I guess God decided my time to leave this world had not yet come.

Life began in earnest for me about five years later when I read *Autobiography of a Yogi* for the first time. I wanted to know more about everything in that book. I understood that Yogananda had founded an organization called Self-Realization Fellowship, but I missed entirely the part about the lessons they send out that could teach me what I wanted to know. So I went to the phone book and looked up "yoga."

This was around 1980, and there wasn't a yoga studio on every corner the way there is now. I found an address in San Francisco, just across the Bay from where I lived. I wasn't that familiar with the city and made a common tourist mistake, going to Seventh Street instead of Seventh Avenue. The Avenues are a quiet residential area. The Streets at that time were something else entirely: mostly a warehouse district, with some unsavory sections you wouldn't want to visit at night.

Fortunately, it was the middle of the day. Somehow the numbers were close enough that, even though I wondered whether I was in the right place, I kept on walking, searching for the yoga place I'd seen in the telephone directory.

It was all warehouses and almost no one else was on the street. I did pass one guy sitting in a stairwell reading some papers. After wandering awhile longer without finding what I was looking for, I went back to speak to him.

When I got close I saw printed on the paper he was reading, "Self-Re-alization Fellowship Lessons." This extraordinary meeting was as much a miracle for that man as it was for me. He was struggling to learn more about Yogananda's teachings; I didn't know where to start. He told me about the lessons, which got me going on the right path. He took our meeting as a sign from Master that despite his own difficulties, he should persevere.

—from Paalaka

FRIENDS *in* HIGH PLACES

The Communist dictatorship ruling Rumania in 1982 banned everything spiritual. Somehow, though, a man named Aman, from Switzerland, came to Bucharest and was allowed to teach Transcendental Meditation. Artists, professors, film directors, and intellectuals of all types took his courses.

Then the dictator Ceausescu began to think his regime would be overthrown by the power of meditation. He instigated a reign of terror against all those who had participated. They were fired from their jobs and reassigned to menial work, even sent out of Bucharest into the countryside. My coworker and I had taken all the classes, and every day we expected to be targeted.

My family and I prayed to St. Anthony of Padua, but without much hope. Everyone we knew was getting sacked. Eventually the turmoil stopped. Of all those who'd taken the classes, we were the only ones who did not lose their jobs.

Seven years later, when the dictator was killed, we found out why we had been saved. The dictator's son, who was not so crazy as his father, was a friend of a friend of my coworker. Given the intensity of the purge, this was too tenuous a connection to warrant special treatment; but the son had issued an order that we were not to be touched.

—from Nora Tomosoiu

LANE CHANGE

Our two cars entered the freeway at the same time, but rush hour traffic soon separated us. In an attempt to keep Eugene's car in sight, I moved over to the fourth lane on the far left. Soon I spotted him about a quarter of a mile ahead, one lane to the right.

There were three car lengths of open space behind him, so I sped up to eighty-five miles per hour to move into the gap. As I came abreast of the car trailing his, I let up on the accelerator knowing that momentum alone would place me safely just where I wanted to be.

Before turning the wheel I checked the distances again. There was plenty of space behind Eugene, and in the rearview mirror I could see the trailing car already fading out of my peripheral vision. All clear.

I turned the wheel about two degrees to the right and felt the beginning of a smooth fade into the next lane. At the same moment I glanced into the right-side-view mirror. A pair of eyes, like a hunted animal cornered in a hollow log, stared back at me.

A fast-moving motorcyclist was heading for the same spot I was about to occupy. I was in the process of turning; we were milliseconds from impact. No time even to alert my wife in the passenger seat next to me. Death was at our side.

In that instant the steering wheel came to a hard stop, as if at the end of its turning radius. My eyes were fixed on the eyes of the motorcyclist reflected in the mirror, but now I could also see his silhouette outside the passenger window. Then the air around us began to fracture. It rippled like water in a pond, disturbed by a stone thrown into its center. The rippling air wrapped itself around the front of the car and pushed it back into the left lane.

The motorcyclist turned his body slightly as he pulled into the lane in front of me, our eyes still locked together. Silently we acknowledged that we had been miraculously spared. Then he turned his head away, sped off down the freeway, and I never saw him again.

—from Richard

HAND *in* HAND

All we know about my father's upbringing is that he lived alone with his grandmother. He was very secretive about why or when his parents left him, and even whether or not they were still alive. Alcoholism apparently figured in there somewhere.

Sometime in his childhood he was struck by a paralytic disease, which weakened the right side of his body. If you looked at him closely, even when he was an adult, you could see it. Still, during his school years he was state champion in tennis, twice. He had tremendous will power when he chose to use it. In college he was a scholar as well as an athlete—handsome, personable, well-liked, definitely a "most likely to succeed" type of man.

He was also, even then, an alcoholic.

For a career he chose to be a Lutheran minister, and through most of my childhood was the assistant pastor of a church in Southern California.

When he married and raised children of his own, he was determined that his would be a model family for the whole congregation. Having no actual experience of what a family should be, he created it from the outside, mimicking what he thought an ideal family should look like.

My parents had a very active social life—bridge parties, square dancing, golf. Everything included alcohol; and my father was always the life of the party, especially when he was drinking. For every social occasion we three children were dressed to the nines, every hair in place. My two brothers are twelve years apart in age, with me, the only daughter, exactly in the middle.

My father saw to it that we were well trained, not only in academics but also in sports—and for me, music and dance. He was an active, involved dad, especially with my brothers and their sports. He also often took me out on the tennis court early in the morning, seeing in me a future champion.

And he sexually abused me; and when he became angry—which was often—he beat my mother.

Finally, when I was twelve, my parents separated and a few years later divorced. Around that time my mother became a fundamentalist Christian, and ever thereafter I had to deal with her unrelenting intensity on that subject.

Growing up with such hypocrisy from a so-called "man of God," then later dealing with my mother's religious fanaticism, should have turned me against God forever.

The first miracle of this story is that they did not. In fact, as my life progressed, I drew closer and closer to God. Looking back I can see that even at the worst of times, even when I let go of His hand, He clung tightly to mine.

Always He provided at least one safe person for me—my older brother, a nurse at my elementary school, a kindly neighbor who welcomed me into his home.

It is no surprise that once I got out on my own I made one unfortunate choice after another. I sought haven in religion, but several times put my faith in spiritual leaders who, although perhaps sincere in their love for God, turned out to be alcoholic, perverted, or self-serving in other ways.

It is no surprise, also, that I sought comfort in men. But I had no insight into people. I married three times, and had several other relationships as well. I never chose a replica of my father, but each man bore enough similarity to him that true selfless love was not possible.

Soon after I married for the first time my father assured me, in the crudest way, that even though I had a husband, "You will always belong to me."

In my mid-thirties, after a painful divorce, I started seeing a therapist. I knew something was very wrong with me, but I had suppressed the memory of most of what happened to me as a child, so the cause of my unhappiness was a mystery to me.

Fortunately, God knew, and he brought me—without my knowing it—to a therapist who specialized in helping people who had suffered in the way I had. And her solution, thanks be to God, was to help her clients come closer to God.

Nothing happened fast, nor did my healing follow a straight and simple course. This is not that kind of miracle. This is the miracle of God's patient love. He never gave up on me, and as a result, I never gave up on myself.

As for my father, for many years he still held a certain terror for me. Even after he was crippled by a stroke, confined to a wheelchair, with the beginning of dementia, I was still afraid to be alone with him. Only when I saw that he could no longer dominate me, physically or emotionally, was I able to be in his presence without fear. In a rare, self-revealing moment, he said, "I went to be with God, but I was never good enough."

Ah, what suffering! It doesn't excuse the suffering he inflicted on me, but it helps explain it; and it gives me greater compassion for what it must have been like for him.

I feel closer now to God than ever before. I have found a spiritual path and a community of like-minded friends, and I live with them a simple life of service and devotion.

The miracle of this story is that I am here to tell it.

—from Anonymous

ON *the* WAY *to* ITALY

"Black ice" was a concept that always held unique terror for me—that thin layer of all but invisible ice on the road that makes driving treacherous. Not that I'd ever seen it, what to speak of driving on it, or suffering any of the myriad tragedies the news media told me it could cause. I grew up in Florida where even the idea of "winter" was pretty foreign.

Later I moved to the West Coast. For many years I've made my home at the Ananda Meditation Retreat in the Sierra Nevada foothills. So by now I've seen my share of ice and snow. My life is fairly self-contained within the Retreat, however, so when the weather is bad I drive as little as possible.

In the year 2000 I felt the guidance to go on an extended trip, starting in Italy. I left in December to drive my truck across the United States, visiting friends and relatives along the way. I planned to leave my truck on the East Coast and fly on to Europe.

Along the way, in the middle of Utah somewhere, the temperature began to drop and it started to snow. I was going down a highway at about sixty-five miles an hour when I found myself in the middle of a convoy of eighteen-wheelers. Their tires kicked up so much powdery snow it was a virtual whiteout. I couldn't slow down to pull over. In those conditions no one would see me and I'd get rammed from behind.

It was too dangerous, though, to stay where I was, so I had to gather my courage and blindly head out into the left lane to get ahead of the convoy. As I sped along, passing truck after truck, the thought of black ice was never far from my mind. Fortunately I made it without mishap and found clear sky, clear road, and, in a manner of speaking, clear sailing. Or so I thought.

Minutes later, my lifelong fear manifested. I hit black ice and my truck began to spin. I knew the convoy of eighteen-wheelers was not far behind, and if I kept on like this, they would plow into me. Time slowed down. Seconds felt like minutes.

"Why is this happening?" I thought. "I'm following Your guidance and going to Italy just as You inspired me to do. This is *not* the plan."

Then it occurred to me to try to gain control of the spinning truck, but I couldn't remember what to do. Do you turn *into* a spin or *away* from it? Do you hit the *brakes* or do you push on the *accelerator*? In Florida they never taught us these things.

To make matters worse, even if I could have remembered, I am a little dyslexic. In those circumstances to figure out which was left and which was right, and then get my brain and hands working together to respond appropriately, seemed a dim prospect indeed.

"Necessity is the mother of invention." Suddenly a creative new idea came to me. I lifted both feet from the pedals and both hands from the wheel.

"Master, this one is yours," I said.

My truck did three high-speed loopity-loops down the middle of the highway. Oddly, I wasn't frightened. It was like a carnival ride. Finally we slid off the road backwards at the only place where there wasn't a ditch. Seconds later, fifteen very large eighteen-wheelers sped by.

Even then I wasn't excited or scared. I felt protected and watched over by a Power greater than me, greater than those trucks, greater than anything this world could throw at me, including black ice.

"Thank you, Master," I said, "for taking such *good* care of me."

Since I was facing forward, I put my truck in gear, pulled onto the highway, and continued my journey. Five minutes later I had to slow down for a major accident. Many cars and big trucks had crashed because of, yes, black ice.

If I had not done my carnival ride at the moment Master had chosen, I would have been right in the middle of it.

—*from Charles Evans*

AUM

Forest fires burn more rapidly going uphill than down. Rising heat and smoke dry and preheat the fuel. When the wind is behind a fire going uphill, it is very hard to stop it.

This was the combination that burned down much of Ananda Village in June 1976. All these years later, we haven't forgotten. So in August 2004, at the end of a long dry summer, when a fire started roaring uphill with the wind behind it, we had no illusions about how dire the consequences might be. Right in its path was a cluster of houses and the Expanding Light Retreat.

Volunteer firefighters in the community, plus untrained residents and many guests, sprang into action to protect a few of the smaller buildings. Air tankers and helicopters began dropping water and fire retarding chemicals on the blaze. Forty trucks and four hundred firefighters arrived in an effort to contain what was rapidly becoming a raging inferno.

"This is the kind of fire that easily gets out of control and burns thousands of acres and hundreds of homes," the fire chief told us.

Community members gathered on the front lawn of the market.

"We were on the other side of the hill from the fire," Devi said later, "a safe quarter mile from the blaze. But with the heat, smoke, noise from the planes, and uncertainty about what might happen next, you could feel the tension grow. The fire felt like a negative psychic force trying to weaken us and make us afraid. There was nothing more we could do to contain the fire physically, but there was much we could do to generate light to overcome the darkness."

Devi organized a prayer circle, starting with about twenty people, soon expanding to fifty or more. Together they visualized the fire itself and all those affected by it: buildings, plants, animals, and people.

Systematically they brought to mind each aspect, surrounding it in light, and praying for well-being, safety, and divine harmony for all. After each prayer they chanted AUM three times. AUM is the all-pervasive vibration of the universe, the substance from which all created things are made.

"At first," Devi said later, "the fire seemed to be winning, its darkness more powerful than our light. Undaunted we prayed on. Chanting AUM over and over again, for two hours we prayed, until finally we felt the darkness being chased away by our ever-expanding light."

Soon after, the fireman coordinating the effort arrived at the market. To our immense relief he announced, "The fire is contained."

Then he went on to say, "You are very lucky. The blaze was racing uphill with the wind behind it toward your retreat and your homes. We were doing everything we could, but I have to say, I didn't see how we could stop it. Then, suddenly, the wind reversed itself! It started blowing the fire *away* from your buildings, back down the hill into the already burned areas. With the wind on our side, and no fresh fuel to feed the fire, we were able to bring it under control."

He paused, then added, "I've never seen that happen before."

Looking at the circle of community members who had been praying for the last two hours, he said, "I don't know what you people did, but whatever it was, it worked."

—from Asha

UNEXPECTED GIFTS

*"God knows what you need,
and will do much more for you than the
best that you can imagine for yourself."*

PARAMHANSA YOGANANDA
~ The Essence of Self-Realization ~

GOD REMEMBERS

 'm frugal by nature. I only spend money on practical things. My house is quite bare—at least some people would describe it that way—not a single knickknack. So I was surprised when I felt drawn to enter the souvenir shop full of the usual touristy things.

Every year my husband and I go from our home in California to Assisi, Italy, to lead a two-week yoga and meditation retreat at Ananda's community there. We've been doing this for a number of years, and many of the same people come every time. By now we have become quite close.

This year the theme was yoga teachings in the Bible. It had been particularly inspiring. We were staying an extra week to relax and enjoy Assisi—to me one of the most spiritual places in the world, made holy by St. Francis and St. Clare.

The uplifting influence of the retreat was still very much with me, so even though the impulse to enter the shop was quite out of character, I felt filled with grace and followed the flow without question.

Glancing around the store, I was drawn to a display of hanging chimes apparently designed for children. Each one included a decorative wooden piece with a painting of an animal. I felt drawn to the one with two kittens, one black and one white. When my hand touched it, an inner voice said, "Buy this for Beate."

Beate was the four-year-old daughter of a woman I used to work with at Ananda Village. After Beate was born, I had little contact with her mother and saw Beate only occasionally. I liked both of them, but there was no special connection between us.

In that uplifted state, though, I didn't question. I bought the chime.

When Christmas came, I gift-wrapped the chimes and put the package in the mailroom, addressed to Beate with a little note from me: "I saw this in Assisi and thought you might like it."

A week later I happened to see her mother. "Beate had two kittens: one black and one white," her mother told me. "A few months ago, both of them died. It made her so sad. But when your gift came, Beate felt that someone had remembered her kittens, and knew how much they meant to her. She was deeply touched and comforted."

—from Diksha

SHOWER of BLESSINGS

"Perfect" is how many people describe the weather in San Francisco. "Monotonous" is what I call it. I grew up in Illinois and didn't move to California until I was nearly thirty. One thing I especially missed was the dramatic summer thunderstorms of my home state.

I was back in Illinois for a reunion of old friends. It was the right season for thunderstorms, but the wrong year. There was a terrible drought: many weeks without rain and no relief in sight. I had never seen the cornfields so distressed.

A friend took me to Winnetka Beach on Lake Michigan.

"What would you like to see on your visit here?" he asked me.

"A good thunderstorm!" I said.

"You are out of luck," my friend told me, reminding me of the drought.

Nonetheless I faced the lake, pumped my fists in the air, and with melodramatic but joyous passion cried out, "Come on, God! *Give me a thunderstorm!*"

Ten minutes later, huge bolts of lightning cracked over the lake from black thunderclouds that now blanketed the sky. The temperature had dropped twenty degrees. The skies opened and rain fell in sheets. We didn't even try to protect ourselves, but just stood there, laughing, soaked to the skin.

After a few minutes it was over. We walked the couple of blocks away from the lake to where our car was parked. The streets there were completely dry.

Next day, a small article in the newspaper described the "freak storm" that had hit Winnetka Beach on Lake Michigan, dropping a half-inch of rain in ten minutes. "Mere blocks away," the article said, "no rain fell."

—from Lynn Lloyd

No?!

always planned to have a child. It was all worked out in my mind how I would raise her. (Usually it was a daughter I visualized.) Freedom was the key: no unnecessary rules or restrictions; freedom of action and self-expression; freedom from stifling, useless social custom. That was my daughter and the mom I would be.

I wasn't going to do it on my own though, so I was always on the lookout for my baby's father. A couple of times I got engaged, but nothing ever came of it. (Thank God!) Finally, when I was thirty-six, the perfect man came into my life. Although we met three thousand miles from where he was born, he had grown up in the town where many of my relatives live. They had known his family for years and thought well of the whole clan.

When he asked me out, I announced, "I am a package deal. I want marriage and a child, and if you are not up for that, there's no pointing in our going out." He was twenty-four years older than me and had already raised two sons. He wasn't thinking about starting a new family; but if that's what I wanted, he wanted it too.

A few years after we got married it was time to get pregnant. As it happened, we had just started taking a yoga and meditation class together. It seemed incidental at the time, but it turned out to be the way of life we have followed ever since.

As part of the meditation, the group leader suggested an exercise. "Hold up to the Divine Light," she said, "whatever question you might have. Then, still your heart and listen for the answer."

"I want to have a child," I said, certain that Whoever was there to receive my question would send back an enthusiastic "Yes!" Instead, however, I immediately heard a loud voice inside my mind saying, "What you are holding up to the Divine is not the divine plan."

This answer was an unequivocal "No." Through the years many of my prayers have been answered, but none in so tangible a way. As far as I can remember, I had never given up a desire without fulfilling it. But to my astonishment, at this sudden dismissal of my lifelong plan, I felt no sadness, regret, or rebellion.

"Of *course*," I thought, "if I were destined to have a child I would have married one of those young men years ago. Now I'm nearly forty and my husband is over sixty. What *could* I have been thinking?"

The sheer egocentricity of my former wish overwhelmed me. It was all about doing a perfect job of raising a child, so that *I* could say *I* had done it. Oops. Not the person I aspired to be; at least, not anymore.

So I let it go. Just like that.

From that point my life with my husband began to flower, leading us step by step to a life at Ananda Village more fulfilling than any I could have imagined for myself, or we could have imagined together.

And the daughter came too: not my own, but the child of a neighbor—my perfect karmic offspring. Her mother is happy to embrace with gratitude the truth that "It takes a village to raise a child."

—*from Devadasi*

Happy Ending

Except for a couple of trips to the emergency room, my ninety-two-year-old mother thought she was doing just fine living on her own in her big house in St. Louis, Missouri—even though none of her children lived nearby. My siblings, both medical professionals, live hours from St. Louis. I live in California.

"She is an accident waiting to happen," my sister said, "but she won't listen to us. You must persuade her that she needs to move someplace where there is more supervision."

I had been concerned; now I was anxious. But what could I do from California? I took my anxiety into meditation and laid it out to Master. "You know my mother. She has such a strong will! If she doesn't want to move, there is nothing I can do about it." A great calmness descended over me, and an inward assurance, "All will be well."

I phoned her immediately. "I know you want to stay where you are," I said to my mother on the phone, "but why don't I come out there and we can research options? That way, when you do feel ready to move, we'll know what's available." She agreed, and I flew out to spend a week with her.

I never urged her to do anything, but always asked, "What do you want?" The assurance I had received in meditation stayed with me, and I was able to just let the situation unfold. By the time I left, seven days later, we had moved her into a small apartment overlooking a garden in an extraordinary independent living facility. She was trying it out for a month. She loved it and decided to stay.

Her greatest dread had always been that she would become incapacitated and end her life in a nursing home. A little less than two years after she moved into the apartment, her body began to fail.

My mother always had lots of energy and will power and was interested in everything. She could be critical and complaining, but she never lacked for zip! Now she had slow internal bleeding, and even with regular trips to the hospital for blood transfusions she was exhausted and confused.

On the eve of yet another hospital stay, the Personal Care Director suggested that she move from independent to assisted living. I called my mother on the phone, and she spoke to me from her hospital bed.

"I have lots of money, but I can't even eat," she said unhappily. Then, to my surprise, she said, "Maybe I should have joined Ananda." I had lived at Ananda Village for nearly forty years. It was the first time she had expressed the slightest inclination toward my way of life.

After the call, I wrote Swami Kriyananda asking him to pray for her. He had met my mother once when she came to visit me at Ananda.

The next day I called her again. "How do you feel?" I asked. She'd had the transfusion.

"Wonderful!" she said, more positive and energetic than I had heard her be in a long time. More than a year before, I'd given her a spiritual book. Her response at that time was caustic. Now she was both reading and enjoying it! In the middle of our conversation, she quoted from the book a saying of Master's: "Conditions are always neutral." (The rest of it, which she didn't say, is, "It is how you react to them that makes them appear sad or happy.")

The only way I can describe the phone call is: Amazing!

Later, when I checked my e-mails, I learned that my request had reached Swamiji, and that he had started praying for her the night before.

After that, every time I spoke to my mother she was bursting with good will and love for all. Even people she had criticized in the past she now saw in a kindly light. Soon I went for a visit.

The change was dramatic. She looked years younger. She was fun, funny, and full of life. She expressed the greatest kindness and appreciation for all. That last month of her life, she was the happiest, most loving I have ever known her to be. At the end, by the grace of God, I was there when she passed peacefully away.

—from Anandi

My Invisible Friend

You may think being addicted to drugs and being a disciple of a great guru are mutually exclusive, but I tell you, from my own experience, they are not.

Naturally, each disciple finds in the teachings of Master those verses that speak personally to him. You won't be surprised to hear my favorite.

"I'm not saying you should do wrong," Yogananda said, "but if you can't help yourself, due to habits that are too firmly rooted, then do it with God. He likes that!"

Even in my worst moments I could still sense that I was not alone. Always I was accompanied by the One I called "my Invisible Friend." His presence, I believe, mitigated many bad karmas that would otherwise have destroyed me.

Finally I reached the nadir of that chapter of my life. One night, alone in the woods, I found myself walking in circles, fervently repeating, "I just can't stop! I just can't stop! I just can't stop!"

Inwardly I heard Master sigh, then somewhat reluctantly say, "All right, then."

A moment later I was surrounded by a squadron of police, who promptly arrested me and took me to jail. Alone in a cold cell, with no one but my Invisible Friend to keep me company, I was astonished to find myself focused on a single thought: my love for God.

Everything had been stripped away—my dignity, my self-respect, and now my freedom—but nothing could come between God and me. That lesson alone was worth all it had cost me to learn it. This was the turning point, the blessing I had been praying for.

"I love you. I love you. I love you," I said over and over again to my Invisible Friend.

A capable attorney managed to delay for six months my appearance before the judge. By that time I had an impressive record of therapy, community service, and clean and sober living. The result was a hand-shake from the judge, congratulating me for turning my life around.

I accepted his congratulations. I had worked hard, but it was a joint effort. Master and me, together.

—from Jack Wallace

LONG WALK HOME

For years now I have been taking seclusion at the Ananda Meditation Retreat. My routine is pretty well worked out: long meditations in the morning; then long walks in the afternoon, often down the steep hill to the river and back up again.

Even when meditation doesn't come easily, I tough it out and put in the hours. So I was a little surprised when, feeling a little restless, I jumped up from meditation early and headed out for the river.

The trail to the river isn't used much, and every year it gets rougher and more overgrown. I'm a strong man and an experienced hiker, so this was an observation, not a concern.

Not far from the river I came to a section of the trail that is just a narrow ledge on a steep hillside, covered with loose slate. The hill forms a wall on one side and a nearly vertical eight-foot drop on the other.

"Hmmm," I thought, "that looks dangerous."

One second later I was flipping around in the air, completely off the ground, sailing over the drop-off. It crossed my mind that my future was at stake, so I looked for some way to mitigate my fate. I found none.

Eventually I hit the ground, then bounced once or twice before coming to rest on a level spot. Perhaps I lost consciousness. I'm not sure.

As soon as awareness returned, I calmly looked around, taking stock of where I was. Next I remember saying, perhaps out loud, and perhaps only to myself, "Thank you, Divine Mother." Of everything that happened, I think that, for me, was the most satisfying moment.

Swami Kriyananda tells of the time he was vacationing by himself in Hawaii. He was alone in his hotel room, with the safety lock engaged, when he dislocated his artificial hip. Suddenly he was in terrible pain and could barely move. He was sitting on the floor when it happened, but with great effort managed to pull himself up onto the bed and, eventually, to reach the bedside phone and call the front desk.

The hotel was on the far side of the island from the hospital, and it took almost an hour for the paramedics to arrive. When they finally got there, Swami couldn't get off the bed to unlock the door for them, so he had to lie there while they broke down the door to get in.

Throughout it all, he told us, he felt nothing but gratitude to Divine Mother for giving him this opportunity to love Her, no matter what happened.

His loving response to such difficult circumstances has always inspired me. I was so pleased that, in such a moment, I responded in the same way.

Few people take the trail down to the river. If I waited for someone to come, it could be a long time before I had any company. No question: I had to walk up the hill I had just spent an hour coming down.

My left hand and arm were useless. My right leg was painful, but didn't appear to be broken. It turned out I had a compression fracture in my pelvis, and that was affecting my leg. My face and scalp were cut pretty badly, and there was blood everywhere, but I could breathe okay and see just fine.

I didn't even ask, "How badly am I hurt?" That information was not useful, so why go there? Only one leg and one arm were working well, on opposite sides of my body, so it was tricky to ascend the vertical wall I had just fallen over. Finally I found a shallower section and somehow scrambled up.

Then it was just putting one foot in front of the other. Yes, there was pain; but much of weakness, I realized, is the confusion of a plethora of choices. Having no choice means that all your energy is directed one-pointedly: in my case, to walk back up that trail.

Later, I estimated the walk took about two hours. Long enough at the time, but not long in the great scheme of things.

When I finally reached the retreat buildings, no one was around. I thought I must look a God-awful mess, so I went first to a bathroom to clean up a little, then over to the dining room.

Nakula was in charge at the retreat. I felt he was the one I needed to find, although he often isn't around the main area. From the dining room I could see that there was a meeting going on in the kitchen, and Nakula was there. I asked another retreat guest to request that Nakula come speak to me.

"We are going to the hospital," Nakula said as soon as he saw me.

To restore my hand and arm took some pretty sophisticated surgery, then months of rehabilitation. I had recently turned sixty-five and signed up for Medicare. If the accident had happened thirty days earlier, I wouldn't have been able to afford the care I needed.

The energy of recovery sapped my meditations for months, and it was a full year before I had the courage to walk down to the river again.

The real gift from the whole experience was finding out that, even when God knocks me over, spins me around, and slams me down again, my heart spontaneously responds, "Thank you, Divine Mother."

—*from Nishkama*

ROAR *of the* LION

I was only three years old and couldn't make clear to my parents the intensity of my nighttime fears. "All children have bad dreams," they thought, and put what I said in that category. I couldn't explain to them that this was different.

Night, for me, was a torment. Usually I would lie awake for hours, afraid to fall asleep. We lived in my grandmother's house in India. Only when I could see the light of dawn through the cracks in the roof tiles would I finally doze off.

I would sleep then until late in the morning. I begged my parents to wake me earlier, but they felt I needed the sleep. Inadvertently, they kept me on the cycle of nighttime sleeplessness, fear, and loneliness.

I had various nightmares, but it was one recurring dream that made me so afraid. It came several times a week.

In it I was a little boy, dressed in shorts, walking barefoot in red dirt with two companions of my own age. It looked like central India, only earlier, when the British were still in charge. In this lifetime I also grew up in that area.

In the dream, my friends and I followed a forest track to a temple we wanted to visit. Two stray dogs started following us. When the dogs came into the dream, the fear would build.

Together we looked around the temple. I had to get home earlier than the other boys, so I went out a back door alone, taking a shortcut through a denser part of the forest.

I heard a lion roar, which frightened me. I began to walk faster.

For me as the dreamer, the lion roar filled me with almost unbearable dread. At the same time, for my dreaming self it was a relief to hear it, for it meant the end of the dream was near. I always knew I was dreaming, but no matter how much will power I exerted, I couldn't change the dream or wake up.

I parted some bushes and came face to face with the lion. At this point the dream always ended, presumably because the lion ate me.

It seems obvious this was a past-life memory, imprinted so fearfully on my subconscious that when my defenses were down, it broke through over and over again. The only solution for me was to try not to sleep.

In many ways the dream was more real to me than waking life. In waking life, every day is different. By contrast, the dream was always the same—the reality of it reinforced by constant repetition.

Finally, when I was seven years old, I had had enough. One night, after going through the unvarying sequence of events and emotions, I didn't wake up, but another part of my sleeping self took over.

I had to face up to the fear! It was time to end this nighttime terror! In my sleep state I prayed intensely to God for help. Then I deliberately called up the dream, something I had *never* had the courage to do before.

This was a mental re-creation rather than the actual dream, so the familiar scenes were slightly different from the usual. I sped quickly through them until I came to the part where the lion appears.

Face to face with the lion, something happened that had never happened before. A sudden blaze of light struck the lion on the side of his head. He turned to face the light, which emanated from a tall, robed figure who illuminated the entire scene.

The figure called to the lion and spoke a few words to him. The lion listened attentively, then trotted tamely away. My fear had been told to go away, and it did.

The figure then turned to me and said telepathically, "Well, that won't bother you again, will it? Well done!"

I didn't know how to respond. I was amazed that my prayer had been answered. At the same time, I thought I was the one who had bravely banished my own fear. After all, hadn't the figure told me, "Well done!"? It didn't occur to me to respond in the obvious way, "Thank you for making the lion go away."

That dream has never bothered me again, nor have I been plagued by any other nightmares.

Banishing the fear, I understand now, entailed not only having the courage to face it, but also putting out the effort to draw the grace of God. For it was that grace, not I, that sent the lion away.

—*from Rashmi*

MOTHERHOOD

I always assumed I would have children, probably four, the same as the family I grew up in. My first marriage ended quickly in divorce, and my second marriage didn't start until my late twenties. My new husband was ambivalent about becoming a father.

Then I went to medical school, and suddenly I was thirty-nine. For the next twelve months every morning started with a discussion between my husband and me about whether we would try to get pregnant.

We were deeply devoted to an Indian guru called Sant Keshavadas, but we never talked to him about the question of becoming parents. I am not sure why. Perhaps I didn't want to have his word on the subject, in case it contradicted mine.

"Guruji," as we called him, was coming from India to Florida. We lived in California but flew to Florida to meet him. Afterwards I was going to Boston to visit old friends and to meet their newborn son, Daniel. They had asked me to be his godmother.

I was extremely anxious about seeing the baby, fearing that my jealousy would mar the otherwise joyous occasion.

When it was time for me to leave, Guruji sent word, "Before you go, come and see me." Alone with me in his room he said, "You are going to Boston to see the child." I hadn't mentioned it to him, but somehow he knew. Then he took my face in his hands, came very close to me, and looked right into my eyes. "When they ask you, say, 'God is my child. Guru is my child.'"

In that moment, the desire to have a baby of my own evaporated and never returned. Later, holding my godson was pure joy, without a trace of longing or envy.

It took more time for me to understand the meaning of what Guruji had said to me. Gradually I came to see that what I thought was the desire to have a baby was really the desire to serve wholeheartedly, in the way a mother does.

Since then God has given me endless opportunities to "mother" Him in friends, relatives, patients in my medical practice, and many other people's children.

—from Shanti Rubenstone

No Introduction Needed

I've always loved animals. I used to take my cat Dirk everywhere with me—even camping in the woods, sleeping in a tent. Often he would explore on his own; but when I called him, he always came running back to me. So I was deeply touched to read about the practice in Mahatma Gandhi's ashram of sending silent love to the animal world as a way of extending man's sympathies beyond his own species.

One night, at the end of a particularly deep meditation, I prayed for all the animals on our planet, bowing to God incarnated in those forms.

Afterwards, I went to a nearby café for a glass of fresh orange juice. It was unusually crowded, but I managed to order my juice and find a place to sit down.

Suddenly a pit bull dog emerged from the crowd. Sometimes that breed can be fearsome, but this dog was not. He jumped onto my lap and started licking my face as if we were old friends, reunited after a long separation! No dog—no animal—has ever shown such an instant liking for me!

When his owner finally caught up with him, he was astonished.

"He tends to be quite suspicious of people," the owner said. "I have *never* seen him greet anyone in this way!"

I believe that, in the great web of consciousness, that dog sensed my prayer and rushed over to say, "Thank you."

—from Darshan

FRIENDS *to the* END

My friend, Happy Winningham, contracted AIDS early in the epidemic, but defied the odds and lived many years longer than anyone expected. She was an actress by profession, and her love of drama was not diminished by her illness. Several times she went to the brink of death, and even into the world beyond, only to return and take up her life more or less as before.

It wasn't easy for her. "Like having a constant case of a bad flu," is how she described her health. But those of us who loved her—and she was loved by many—were grateful for the extra months and years we had together.

This time, however, it was much worse than anything we had seen before. She had been in a coma for days. Her organs were shutting down, and the resulting swelling and discoloration made her almost un-recognizable.

Happy had deep faith in God and no fear of death. She had been to the other side and knew the light and bliss she would find there. She had fought the good fight and, as her friends, we were willing to let her go.

This was more than a theoretical question for me. Happy had given me medical power of attorney, and now I had to decide whether to disconnect her from the machines that were keeping her alive. This was my last act of friendship for her and I was determined to get it right.

Providentially, Happy had written down some very specific instructions, including that if she went into a coma, we should wait a week before making a decision. After only a few days though, her father, the ethics counselor at the hospital, and even some of the nurses, all felt it was time to take her off the machines. We had several heated discussions. As the sole decision-maker, the pressure on me was intense.

Fortunately, her personal doctor, who had treated Happy for years, thought we should wait. So did all of Happy's friends.

Late in the evening of the fifth night of the coma, my wife Ann and I, Happy's sister, and a few close friends, went to the chapel to pray, asking God for a clear answer about whether to stop the life support.

About midnight, a great peace descended. We had our answer. It was time to let her go.

As we were heading for the ICU to inform the doctor of our decision, Happy's sister asked if we could wait until morning so that Happy's father could be with her at the end. It had taken so long to get clarity, though, that I didn't want to let the moment slip away. But I couldn't say no. I am a father. If it were my daughter, I would want to be there.

Ann and I went back to the hotel to get a few hours' rest. We were sound asleep at 3:00 a.m. when the hospital called. Happy had come out of her coma. As I hung up the phone I saw that Ann, who is the most grounded person I know, had an extraordinary look on her face.

"I just saw Happy," she said. "It wasn't like a dream. She was wearing her bathrobe, standing right there." Ann pointed to a spot not far from our bed.

"Happy kept saying, 'You should have gotten it done. You should have gotten it done,'" Ann told me.

Her words were like a knife to my heart. I should have gotten it done. We all knew at midnight that the time had come. I felt I had failed in the responsibility Happy had given me.

We spent most of that day huddled around her bedside, watching Happy breathe on her own. She even spoke a few words—mostly just getting her bearings, trying to figure out where she was and what had happened. Once again she had defied the odds. But it was going to be a tough road to recovery.

The next morning at 3:00 a.m., once again we were awakened by a call from the hospital. This time, Happy was dying—fast. We rushed over, but after four hours she was still holding on. Her father and step-mother were by her bed. Happy seemed at peace, and I felt my part was done. I was so exhausted I could hardly keep my eyes open.

I went back to the chapel. As soon as I sat down I fell fast asleep. The next thing I knew, the loudspeaker in the chapel was blaring "Code Blue in room 321! Code Blue!" That was not Happy's room number, and she was definitely a "No Code" patient (meaning "Do Not Resuscitate"), but in my stupor I thought they were announcing that Happy was dying.

I ran from the chapel and fell in line behind a doctor rushing to respond to the code. He swiped his identity card on the ICU door and I slipped in behind him. As soon as he was inside, the doctor realized he was in the wrong room and rushed out again.

A minute or two after I arrived, Happy took her last breath. Her father was there, and with tears streaming down his face he said to her again and again, "You go to heaven now. You go to heaven now."

Happy's passing was one of the most beautiful, peaceful experiences of my life. Such a feeling of holiness! I wept with gratitude at the privilege of being with her in those last moments.

Earlier that day the nurses offered to put an oxygen mask on Happy. Her sister immediately said, "Yes." Gently I reminded her that we had decided not to interfere anymore with the process of dying. So the answer was "No."

Happy had chided me, through Ann, for not acting immediately to take her off life support when the guidance was clear. But just denying the oxygen was so difficult. I felt Happy's last act of friendship was to choose the moment of her death, thus sparing me from making the decision for her.

—from Michael Gornik

MAKE RICH *the* SOIL

Mostly I think of myself as a good person. I am a doctor and through medicine have helped many people. I am generous by nature. As a child I told my mother that I would make a lot of money in my life, but I would never have much myself, because whatever I made I would give away or use to help others. And I have been true to my word. I am deeply spiritual and have always tried to live a life that is pleasing to God.

Still, I haven't always lived up to my own high ideals. And on this particular day, in the middle of a three-week period of seclusion, all I could remember were the things I had done wrong.

Starting with my childhood, I recalled the lies I had told my mother, and the times I wouldn't share my toys. In high school, deliberately taking from my friend the boy she wanted, and mocking a teacher who had criticized my work. Then, later, a serious betrayal of the man who had loved me, and who deserved far better than I had given.

On and on it went this way for three days. I made lists of all my mistakes. Some part of me knew this whole exercise was folly, but I was obsessed and couldn't stop myself.

Finally I began to wonder if I even deserved the life I had chosen: to be a doctor; to live in a spiritual community; perhaps to be a minister to others on the path I followed. I began to think God saw it all as mere presumption.

Not knowing what else to do, I went to my meditation room and told God, "I am not getting up from this meditation seat until you tell me, in no uncertain terms, what I am supposed to do. If You know I am unqualified for what I aspire to, then just tell me. No riddles. Just clear, straight answers."

Hour after hour I sat there. I would not get up for food or water until God answered my prayer. Periodically I renewed my entreaty, just in case God had forgotten for a moment that I was waiting for His answer.

After most of a day, I picked up a small book by a Buddhist teacher, Chogyam Trungpa, called *Meditation in Action*. In his colorful way, he had titled one chapter *The Manure of Experience*.

In it he explained how the unskilled farmer throws away his own rubbish, but then has to buy manure from his neighbors. The skilled farmer saves all his rubbish. Despite the smell and the mess of it, he works with it until it becomes something of great value. Spread on his land, or sold to other farmers, it is the foundation for bountiful, nourishing crops.

In the same way, the author went on to explain, the unskilled devotee tries to throw away the experiences of *samsara* (wordly delusion) and just search for *nirvana* (spiritual enlightenment). By contrast, the skilled devotee acknowledges, accepts, and works with all these so-called "negative" things, until they become the fertilizer for the sprouting seed of realization.

"Ah, Lord," I whispered quietly. "Now I understand."

—*from Shanti Rubenstone*

WHY ME?

I didn't know, from one day to the next, what I would be able to do. I always meditated, but I never knew when I would have the energy to do it. Sometimes it was early in the morning; sometimes it was well past noon. That was life with my constant companions, Chronic Fatigue Syndrome and Fibromyalgia.

I had moved to Ananda Village. The teachings and spiritual environment certainly made it easier to cope with my unreliable body. Still, I struggled.

One Sunday, Swami Kriyananda had just returned from Italy and was giving the morning service for the first time in many months. With all my heart I wanted to be there. I was intensely disappointed when I woke up with the worst of my symptoms—like a terrible flu, except it is a chronic condition.

Sitting on the edge of my bed, not having the strength yet to stand, I tried to be brave; but courage failed me. Tearfully I prayed to Master, "Today of all days, why am I so unwell? I do so want to see Swamiji!"

In answer to my prayer, an inner voice said, "In a previous life you committed suicide." A fragment of that incarnation passed before my eyes. My current family members were my children then. We lived together in a village which was invaded by fierce enemies. They were all killed. In despair, I took my own life.

The present illness, I realized, was the necessary balance to that incarnation. The grief that drove me to suicide was understandable, and I could feel God's compassion. Still, I had thrown away the privilege of human life, and the karmic consequence was that it would not so lightly be returned to me.

This was a personal revelation, I hasten to add, not a universal explanation of why others might have this same condition. Each person must understand for himself his own karmic lesson.

This explained a peculiarity of my childhood. I had always felt responsible for the safety and wellbeing of my parents and three siblings. Even as a young child I felt I had to protect them from a lurking threat I could never identify.

In this lifetime my father committed suicide. He was a professor, a dear and wonderful man, who was forced to give up his teaching career when he reached the mandatory retirement age for his university. Lonely and without purpose, he fell into a deep depression and took his life. It was a terrible shock.

Now I understood that God wanted me to experience the pain suicide inflicts on others. After this revelation I tried to learn as much as I could of the Self-realization teachings about suicide, karma, and reincarnation.

Suicide is a plunge into the darkness. The antidote is to live in the light. Soon that became my life purpose and my way of coping with my condition: moment-to-moment, day-by-day, living in the light.

Suicide is an act of supreme ingratitude. God gives us life, and with it, the opportunity to know Him. Yes, He tests us, sometimes greatly;

but He is no tyrant. With every test comes His blessing; the greater the test, the greater the potential blessing.

Everything I read about gratitude struck a deep chord within me. Gratitude itself became a way for me to stay in the light.

There was no miracle healing for me, but in almost miraculous ways more effective treatments came to me. What had been my constant companions, Chronic Fatigue Syndrome and Fibromyalgia, now intrude on my life only occasionally. While I don't exactly welcome their infrequent visits, I accept with gratitude whatever God sends.

—from Anonymous

CONSCIOUS CONCEPTION

By the time my wife and I decided we wanted to have a third child, I was deeply dedicated to my spiritual life. Among other things, I was "practicing the presence of God": an effort to remember God every moment of every day. No matter what you are doing outwardly, you keep the company of God in your heart.

I loved my first and second children with all my heart, but neither showed much inclination for the spiritual path. "Lord," I prayed, "let this third child love You as I do."

Even when my wife and I were making love, I kept practicing the presence, and praying that the child who came to us would have a spiritual disposition. I was aware of the moment of conception, and felt inwardly, "Your prayer has been answered."

The son that was born to us has always been deeply spiritual. When he was old enough I taught him to meditate, suggesting that five to ten minutes would be enough at the beginning. He sat down and focused deeply for almost an hour with no apparent effort. He is still a young man, but so far he seems to have the spiritual disposition I prayed for.

—from Anonymous

ARRANGED MARRIAGE

My son grew up in an Ananda community and respected the teachings of Paramhansa Yogananda. But when "Randy" was able to move out on his own, he wanted to experience a different life. He went to the ski slopes in the winter and to Hollywood in the summer.

I knew his life direction would be greatly influenced by the woman he married. So for years I prayed that Randy's future wife would be spiritually minded and that her path would be compatible with the teachings of Ananda.

At one point, Randy was feeling down and out because of a lost relationship. To encourage him, I told him about the prayer I had been doing to draw to him the right spouse.

"Stop praying like that!" he said, in a way that brooked no contradiction. "I don't want you to interfere with my karma! Just send me light."

I was a little annoyed at not being able to pray directly for something so important. But if I went against his expressed wish, it could create spiritual static in my prayer and disharmony in our relationship.

The brightest and happiest picture I had of him had been taken at the Self-Realization Temple in Hollywood. No coincidence, I thought.

I put a framed copy on my altar with these words in front of it: *Father, I place my son's hand firmly in Thine for Thy keeping.*

This was quite neutral, as he had requested, but happened to be an adaptation from the Ananda Wedding Ceremony, spoken or sung on behalf of the bride's father after he walks his daughter down the aisle to meet her husband-to-be. In this way I honored my son's instruction, but also kept a fragment of my prayer for a spiritually minded wife.

I also made up new words for one of Swami Kriyananda's melodies and sang it often: *Birds fly high up in the sky, as my thoughts for my son Randy. In his heart and in his home, live only Light and Beauty.*

A couple of years went by in this way. He was now living in Los Angeles year-round. Eventually he found a girlfriend he deeply loved. He invited me to meet her, and we had a great time taking in all the sights.

The Ananda Center was not far from where they lived and, as it happened, Swami Kriyananda was speaking, so we all went to hear him.

Sitting with my son and his girlfriend, listening to Swamiji speak, I couldn't hold back the tears of gratitude. I noticed she was crying too.

"Oh dear," I thought, "she is so empathic she is reflecting my feelings!"

After the service ended, I asked her, "Why were you crying?"

"I love Swamiji so much. I want to live at Ananda, but I don't know how that can ever happen," she said.

My jaw dropped in disbelief. Somehow I managed to stammer out, "Where did you come from?!" Then we fell into each other's arms, laughing.

God answered my un-prayed prayer. She and my son now live together in an Ananda community.

—*from Anonymous*

SHOES ON, SHOES OFF

"Put on your shoes!" was the inner prompting, which I chose to ignore. We had just completed our annual yoga retreat in Kerala, India, and I had a romantic notion this last day to stand barefoot on "Mother India" while doing my daily exercises at the edge of the Arabian Sea.

Afterwards I was standing quietly on the grass when I felt something bite the sole of my foot. I glanced at it, saw nothing notable, and put it out of my mind.

A few hours later, when we boarded the plane back to America, I noticed that my shoe felt tight on the foot that was bitten. By the time we reached Singapore four and a half hours later, the foot was hot, swollen, and red.

Halfway through the next ten-hour flight, the leg was hot, red, and swollen almost to the knee. I called the flight attendant, who put a message on the intercom, "Is there a doctor on board?"

Fortunately there was. He thought I was having an allergic reaction to a bee sting, gave me an antihistamine, and arranged for me to lie down and elevate my leg for the rest of the trip.

By the time we landed I could barely walk. Between the pain and the intense itching it was almost two weeks before I got a good night's sleep.

"Next time," I resolved, "I'll listen."

But I didn't.

A few years later I was organizing my closet when I picked up a new pair of walking shoes I had recently acquired. I was admiring how classy they looked when a voice inside gently suggested, "Give them away."

Even though I heard the message loud and clear, I pretended nothing had happened, finished the closet, and went on with my day.

The next morning, getting ready to take the ten-minute walk to work, I picked up the new shoes and responded with some emotion to the inner message of the day before.

"These are great shoes!" I inwardly declared. "I don't earn that much money, and I paid a lot for these. I can't give them away!"

To emphasize my point, I put them on and walked out the door.

"See," I said to God as I returned home at the end of the day, "These are a great pair of shoes."

Early the next morning, on my way to meditate in the community temple, again I chose to wear them.

Two minutes later I hit a stone on our gravel driveway and twisted my ankle so badly that, like a cartoon character, I saw stars. I had to crawl back home on my hands and knees.

For a week I couldn't put any weight on that ankle. For a month I couldn't exercise. It took many treatments and adjustments before I could properly use the foot again.

A few months later a chiropractor friend came to visit. Without comment, I showed her the shoes.

"Give them away," she said.

"Why?!" I asked.

She pointed out all the ways in which they were entirely unsuitable for me—the general structure, the height of the heel, the lack of support.

"If you trip on a stone in this shoe," she told me, "it will severely strain the ligaments of your ankle."

Ah.

It was a year and half before my foot was back to normal. The scar tissue remains as a constant reminder: "When God speaks, listen"

—from Diksha

HE KNOWS YOUR NEED

If I had joined a Christian monastery, it would have been an easier choice for my parents to accept. My mother was a devout Episcopalian. My father didn't share her faith, but he respected her devotion, and at times even accompanied her to church. But my destiny lay elsewhere, on ground unfamiliar to them, with an Indian guru, in the Hindu-Yoga tradition.

I was only twenty-two years old, not yet fully fledged. My parents had been supportive, but concerned, as they watched me seek in vain for my path in life. I had dropped out of college to be a playwright, then dropped writing to search for Truth.

My father was a geologist for Esso, and in the summer of 1948, his company sent him to Egypt to look for oil. My mother stayed back to close up our house. In September, I put her on a ship to go and join him.

That very day, I went to a bookstore in uptown New York City, where I found *Autobiography of a Yogi*, by Paramhansa Yogananda. I read it straight through, scarcely taking time to eat or sleep. I had found my Guru and took the next bus from New York to Los Angeles to become his disciple.

Most of a lifetime later, the wisdom of that decision is self-evident. From my parents' perspective, when eventually they found out, it seemed hasty at best, and at worst, lunatic.

I was strong-minded, but respectful of my parents, and as much as possible, an obedient son. My will was set to become Yogananda's disciple, but could it have been undermined by my parents' disapproval? Fortunately, it was never put to the test. God took them out of the picture altogether.

By the time I saw them again two years had passed. The hope that impelled me to move so quickly had matured into a certainty that nothing could shake.

Fourteen years later, my parents' presence, rather than their absence, played an equally important role in my spiritual life.

Three and a half years after I became his disciple, Paramhansa Yogananda passed away. His immediate successor died three years later and the leadership of his organization came into the hands of a group of nuns. The women found my creativity impossible to deal with. ("Why doesn't he just wait to be told what to do?" they asked one another.)

I, by contrast, was bewildered by what seemed to me their lack of imagination in carrying out the mission our Guru had left in their hands. Finally, in July 1962, I was summoned to a meeting with them in New York City, the same place where I first found *Autobiography of a Yogi* and my life path was set.

The purpose of the meeting was to dismiss me from the organization to which I had given my life. I had no thought of leaving, so for me it was an intensely painful meeting. "Take any job that comes along," was the only advice they gave me. That I had pledged my life to serving my Guru meant nothing to them.

I knew no one in New York; for the last four years I had been serving our work in India. Their hope was to strand me three thousand miles from our headquarters in Los Angeles.

God, however, had plans for me.

When I needed for my parents to be far away, God took them to Egypt. When I needed them close by, amazingly, the very day I was dismissed they arrived in New York City from Europe. They had a home now in California and were planning to drive across the country in a car they had brought with them on the ship. Naturally, they welcomed me as a passenger, and happily allowed me to live with them until I was able to feel my Guru guiding me in my continued service to him.

—from Swami Kriyananda

No More Tears

I was pregnant with our first child when my husband left me. I continued my daily meditation practice, but calmness eluded me. Mostly I just sat in front of the altar and sobbed. Even after the baby was born, this was my daily routine.

Then one day I sat to meditate and actually meditated! It seemed so natural, I didn't even think about it until the meditation was almost over. Then I realized that for the first time in eight months I hadn't cried. In fact, I hadn't even thought about my husband.

It was so remarkable, I wrote down the date and time. I never cried about him again.

Soon after, I received a letter from my husband's friend. It was the only letter he ever wrote to me. The two men were together in India, visiting the ashram of the great woman saint, Anandamayi Ma.

The friend told me that my husband had had a long private interview with "Ma," as the saint is called. In the course of that conversation, my husband told her everything about his life, including how he had abandoned me and our newborn child.

The friend mentioned the date and time of the interview. It was the same day the karma was lifted from me.

—from Anonymous

EMERGENCY CARE

I think every new doctor who prays asks God for the same thing. "*Please*, God, don't let my inexperience cause anyone to be hurt or die." I added to that, "Especially not a child." In medical school, I received little training in how to handle pediatric emergencies, because if you aren't specializing in the care of children, it doesn't happen that often.

Six months after finishing my internship, I was working in a hospital emergency room. It was a hot afternoon in the middle of summer. The ambulance driver called. He was about an hour away, bringing in two near-drowning victims: small boys who had been swimming in a lake. At that point, the connection broke. I had no idea what care they had received or what shape they were in. I couldn't reach the ambulance driver, and he didn't call back.

This was my worst fear. I phoned the backup doctor, but in emergency pediatrics he had no more experience than I did. It was a long hour: taking care of other patients; mentally reviewing everything I knew about children drowning; repeating my prayer, "*Please*, God, don't let anyone be hurt because of my inexperience."

Finally the ambulance arrived. One boy was sitting up smiling, the other boy looked like he was going to be okay. Coming in with them was a man about my age, dressed in swimming trunks with sandy bare feet. He was, like me, a new doctor, a resident at a nearby teaching hospital. His specialty? *Pediatrics*.

He had been swimming at the lake when the near-drowning happened. He climbed into the ambulance with the children, and by the time they got to me, he had already taken care of them.

—from David Kessler

NEW FLIGHT PLAN

I was on an airplane flying eastward across the United States when the direction of my life changed completely. I am a creative person, artistic and spiritual by nature. I came to Ananda in my late teens, and since then my life has been dedicated to serving God as a disciple and a minister. Over the years I have channeled my energy into many different areas of creative service. One by one, however, all those doors had now closed.

Sitting on the airplane, suspended as it were between heaven and earth, I prayed, "Divine Mother, what do You want me to do?"

Immediately, unexpectedly, a thought came with sparkling clarity.

First, let me give you a little background.

Paramhansa Yogananda said that Abraham Lincoln had been a great yogi in past lives who died with a desire to help bring racial equality. Thus his incarnation as the president of the United States who emancipated the slaves. Lincoln was a great man in many ways, but he never received the public acclaim he deserved. He was praised by some, but criticized also by many.

Later, the soul that was Lincoln reincarnated as Charles Lindbergh, the man who first flew solo across the Atlantic Ocean and gained worldwide acclaim for doing so. The progression from Lincoln to Lindbergh is certainly not an obvious one! Only a master like Yogananda could declare such a relationship. As Lindbergh, Yogananda explained, Lincoln received the universal acclaim he deserved but did not get in his earlier incarnation.

All of this I knew before that moment on the plane. But now it took on profound personal meaning.

Almost audibly, the thought was in my mind, "The lives of Lincoln and Lindbergh are well-chronicled. Why don't you study their histories for evidence that what Yogananda said was true?"

Karma and reincarnation are fundamental to the teachings of Self-realization which I had studied thoroughly in my years at Ananda. Lately, though, I felt as if Divine Mother had been giving me a personal crash course in how these principles express in daily life. For several years, and virtually on a daily basis, my experiences, and the reflections they prompted in meditation, had made me somewhat of an expert on the subject. I had been preparing myself for this assignment without knowing it.

Following the plane flight, I dove into this new project. I spent ten years researching what became *The Reincarnation of Abraham Lincoln*. And I was amazed to uncover nearly five hundred examples of the connection between the two men and their shared connection to the path of yoga.

Working on this book not only provided an answer to my prayer, it set in motion a trajectory I have been following ever since.

I became a published author and a recognized authority on karma and reincarnation. I vastly improved my writing skills, which has led to further interesting assignments. Learning how to publish and promote books opened doors to worthwhile service to other authors.

All from a simple and heartfelt question asked of the One who had the answer.

—from Richard Salva

Doctor Shanti

I already had a successful career as a nurse working with one of the best-known cardiologists in the country; helping him with his clinic, surgery, and research; even writing papers on my own. But it wasn't enough. As a young woman I had wanted to be a doctor, but my mother, who never had much faith in my potential, laughed outright when I told her. She assured me I could never make it through medical school, and I didn't have the confidence then that I could prove her wrong.

"Be a nurse," she said. "You'll be lucky if you can manage that." She was a good woman in many ways, but where I was concerned, that goodness was often withheld.

Now, years later, I wanted to finish what I started and get a Ph.D. or an M.D. I moved to a small town in Southern California and started taking a few classes. I had graduated from nursing school, but not from college. I used to run by the ocean, and one of my favorite spots was called *Swami's Beach*. I didn't know at the time that it was named after Paramhansa Yogananda, who before he was *Paramhansa* was called *Swami*. That beach was right next to his seaside hermitage.

Often when I was there, funny things would happen to me. I couldn't just sail past Swami's Beach the way I could any other. Often I would have to slow down, or even sit for a while. One time when I was sitting there, an inner voice spoke with irresistible power.

"You *have* to be a physician. You will need to go to a top Ivy League medical school because you will practice in unusual ways and you'll need this for credibility."

I am capable, but I have never been "school smart." Still, there was no counterthought to this one. Without hesitation I applied to medical school at Harvard, Yale, Duke, Stanford, and a couple of others easier to get into. I had faith in what I had been told, but felt I should also be practical.

Stanford and Yale accepted me outright. Duke put me on their wait list. Harvard said no. I chose Stanford and had a great four years. I was only an average student, but I excelled in other ways. I was a natural with the patients and a leader among the students. When graduation came, I was chosen to give the student address and introduce the guest speaker.

A few days before the ceremony, the dean of the Medical School called me into his office. We had become good friends.

"We can't find your undergraduate degree," he said to me.

"I don't have one," I replied.

"That's *impossible*," he said. "We would *never* accept a student who didn't have a college degree. Furthermore, we can't give you your M.D. unless you already have your B.A."

Even though he spoke forcefully, I wasn't the slightest bit flustered. By that time I had become a disciple of Paramhansa Yogananda and felt it was he who had spoken to me on Swami's Beach that day. The dean was not in charge of my medical career; Yogananda was.

"Well," I said, "you do have a problem. You are in good company, though. Duke and Yale also accepted me without a degree." Then I spoke forcefully, "I *am* going to graduate with my class. It is up to you to figure out how."

In the end, in order to graduate me from medical school, Stanford first had to graduate me from college. They created a Bachelor of Medical Science degree. I am the only person in the history of the school to receive one.

—from Shanti Rubenstone

IT IS ALL ARRANGED

When I went to India in 1972, Divine Mother was my traveling companion. In every situation I asked first of Her, "What do You want?"

I flew from New Delhi to Calcutta to see old friends, hoping also to go further south to Bubaneswar to visit Dr. Mishra, an Indian friend I had gotten to know at the University of California at Davis. But I had no idea how to reach him. No address, no phone number, just the name of the city where he lived.

In Calcutta, two young men were to meet me at the airport, but they were nowhere to be seen. In such a situation, the obvious response would be to rush to the telephone to try to contact the missing friends or arrange things for oneself. Instead I turned calmly inward and asked Divine Mother, "What have You got in mind?"

Hardly two seconds later a passenger from another flight, a man I had never seen before, stopped and asked me, "What is your good name?" (That is how people in India ask, "Who are you?")

When I told him, he replied, "I thought you must be he. I have seen photographs of you in an album shown to me by my friend, Dr. Mishra."

"Dr. Mishra!" I exclaimed. "I have wanted to meet him. Can you give me his address?"

"No need," he replied. "I have come to Calcutta to see him! He is staying here just now. I can take you to him."

And so I got to meet my friend. My other friends had been delayed by traffic and it wasn't until the next day that we caught up with each other.

As it happened, all the habitable hotels in the city were booked that night. Dr. Mishra happily provided a place for me to stay. If I had had to find accommodations I would have been unsuccessful.

Divine Mother knew and made Her own arrangements for me.

—*from Swami Kriyananda*

TRAVEL PLANS

I had already vowed to myself, "If Swami Kriyananda ever tells me to do something, I will do it. No matter what."

So when he said, "I would like it very much if you would visit me in India," I didn't hesitate. "Yes, Sir. I will come." I gave my word to Swamiji, but through him I felt I was giving my word to God.

I was struggling to maintain myself financially as a yoga and meditation teacher. Many times I could barely make the rent on our small center. I could have earned money in other ways, but teaching was my *dharma*—my calling from God. I didn't think it would work out to break one promise to God in order to keep another.

Plans for the trip expanded, and pretty soon it was a group pilgrimage from our center with me as the leader. I still didn't have the money, but the trip was months away. There seemed plenty of time to work things out.

One woman signed up to go and said she also wanted to pay for someone else who couldn't afford it. She asked me to make the arrangements. I asked around, but surprisingly, no one seemed to feel that money was the only obstacle to going. I told the friend who was organizing the trip about the offer, but he didn't have anyone to suggest either. I refused to use my position to take the money for myself.

Those were very difficult months. Money was scarcer than ever. There were some tough interactions with people. I was at the end of teaching a twenty-eight-week course. The man organizing the pilgrimage kept pressing me for the deposit. Soon, he said, he would have to give my place to someone else. I had given Swamiji my word, but I didn't know how I would keep it.

I live in Southern California, and Master's body is buried at Forest Lawn Cemetery in Glendale. In times of need, I seek shelter at his crypt.

On the way I passed a seedy-looking auto parts store. I had the feeling I needed to go in there, but why? I couldn't think of a reason, so I drove on. I spent hours chanting and meditating at the crypt. At the end I felt reassured, but I still didn't know how anything would resolve.

This time, passing the auto parts store, I heeded the inner prompting and pulled into the parking lot. *Maybe I'll just use the bathroom.* The girl at the counter directed me to a grubby room at the back. The walls were covered with the crudest kind of graffiti. Suddenly, right at eye level, I saw something no larger than the message in a fortune cookie: "Be steadfast in the work of the Lord and know your labor is not in vain."

I began to cry. "He knows. He *knows*. No matter what happens, I won't give up."

Later I found the full verse, 1 Corinthians 15:58: "Therefore, my beloved brethren, be ye steadfast, unmoveable, always abounding in the work of the Lord, for as much as ye know that your labor is not in vain in the Lord."

After class that night, the woman who wanted to sponsor someone for the India trip handed me an envelope with $3,100 inside, the full cost of the pilgrimage. "For you," she said. "Not from me. It's from Master. He told me to give it to you. Take it, and don't ever talk to me about it again."

—from Turiya

ROSE SONG

Leaving a marriage after twenty-five years is not easy, especially when children are involved. I had thought long and hard, and prayed deeply about it. Still, when I finally moved out I was sad and scared.

I had rented an apartment for my daughter and me in the Ananda community. As a welcoming gift, someone had put pictures of Master and Swamiji on the kitchen counter, each one encircled with red rose petals.

On our spiritual path, roses are sacred. On special occasions, we shower people with rose petals to represent the blessings of God and the Gurus. The words to a much-loved chant used on holy occasions are *Roses to the left, roses to the right, roses front and behind*—meaning "Guru's blessings everywhere."

Looking at the pictures, I was overcome by conflicting emotions: gratitude, fear, doubt, grief, confusion, hope, and loneliness. Above all, I felt oddly numb, especially in my head and heart. The next day a friend came over with a housewarming gift: a dozen red roses. They were beautiful and warmed my heart, and my scantly furnished apartment.

A week later my daughter and two of her friends had a coming-of-age ceremony. Dressed in long gowns, they danced and sang. They were anointed with holy water, and showered with red rose petals brought by my daughter's godmother.

The following week a patient at the clinic where I work gave me a thank you gift. This has never happened before or since. It was a dozen red roses.

"Oh, Divine Mother," I thought, "You are reassuring me in so many ways. Still, I am uncertain if I am doing the right thing in leaving my marriage to live my truth with You. May I ask for just one more sign?"

She gave me two.

A few days later I went to a favorite Chinese restaurant for lunch. The usual vases of mixed flowers had been changed. At every table now were red roses!

Christmas came, and a friend invited me to her home. Her father is from India, but he lives and teaches in Japan, which is my home country. We gathered around the piano while he played, and we sang songs together in Japanese. What joy to share the holy season with good friends, singing together in my native language, and to feel God's presence in my heart!

In the middle of a song, *Baraga Saita*, I was awestruck to realize that Divine Mother was reassuring me once again. In English, the title would be *A Rose Has Blossomed.*

> *A rose has blossomed.*
> *A rose has blossomed.*
> *It is a bright red rose.*
> *A rose has blossomed in my barren yard.*
> *Just one rose that blossomed is a small rose.*

It brightened up my barren yard.
Rose, rose, little rose,
Do stay blooming forever there.

The rose has died.
The rose has died.
It was a bright red rose.
My yard is again as barren as before.
Though the rose in my yard is gone,
A rose has blossomed in my lonesome heart.
Rose, rose, in my heart,
Do stay blooming forever there.
A rose has blossomed.
A rose has blossomed.
It is in my heart.
It is the bright red rose that will never die

—from Yoko

ACTIONS SPEAK
LOUDER *than* WORDS

A friend of mine was an alpinist and made many first ascensions in Europe. One day he climbed a mountain that, viewed from below, had seemed feasible. He had nearly reached the summit, when, standing on a narrow ledge, he realized it was impossible to climb any further. Above him the mountainside sloped *outward*, forming a final lip. To get over it he would have to go upside down for a little time, hanging over space. Without specialized equipment, of which he had none, it was quite impossible!

It was equally impossible, however, to climb back down the steep cliff he'd ascended. Barely possible to ascend, retreat would have meant looking down to see where to place each footstep. Again: Quite impossible!

Faced with this utterly hopeless situation, he told himself, "I might as well die trying as die here from starvation and exposure!" He set out, therefore, to make the impossible ascent. As soon as his body reached the beginning of that outward curve, he fell back onto the ledge. Well, what else was there to do? He tried again. Then yet again. How many "yet agains" he attempted he could not say exactly, but the number was more than twenty.

"Yet again": Suddenly, at the point where his body had always fallen, a force pushed him against the mountainside, and held him securely there. The force continued to hold him until he had climbed over the lip of rock, and reached the summit. From that point, it was easy for him to walk down the slope on the other side.

Not every prayer is vocalized. Sometimes it is simply the urgent sense of need one feels in times of desperation—provided one's thoughts are offered upward, to God. My friend's prayer was his uplifted courage in the face of absolute and inevitable defeat. Perhaps even the need to continue *upward* brought that sense of mental upliftment that is the essential ingredient of effective prayer.

—from Swami Kriyananda about his friend
Arne Lipovec (Brother Premamoy)

FOLLOW ME

*"Everything in future will improve
if you are making a spiritual effort now."*

SRI YUKTESWAR
~ Autobiography of a Yogi ~

LONG WAY AROUND

The first time I looked into Paramhansa Yogananda's eyes, I was nine years old. It was "only" a photograph, but I felt as if he were standing in front of me, arms raised in blessing.

My parents had brought me for the first time to the Ananda temple in Palo Alto, which is not far from where we lived. Before that we had gone to a Catholic church, which I never enjoyed. I had a natural connection with God. When I was a small child, my mother says, I used to sit out in the backyard with our pets and sing little prayers I made up myself. I felt God's love and joy out in Nature, not sitting in a pew in the middle of an enormous building. Nothing about that church made me feel close to Him.

The Ananda temple at that time was still a "storefront church," operating out of rented rooms in an office building. I found this a little strange. Both my parents worked in offices, so I thought of them as places of business, not a place for God. But I was open to letting things unfold. For the first part of the service I wasn't with my parents in the sanctuary, but in a nearby children's room. The family across the street had introduced us to Ananda, and both those children were there. So I was welcomed by friends.

The adult in charge settled us in front of the altar and began to tell us about the pictures of the Masters there. I was attracted to all of them, but Yogananda mesmerized me. Looking into his eyes, I felt I was in the presence of God.

When it was time to go into the sanctuary to receive an individual blessing as part of the Festival of Light, I followed the other children without any idea where we were going or why. When I stepped into the sanctuary, I felt bathed in warmth and joy. The lights were dim. There were music and candles everywhere; and on the altar, the same picture of Master.

As I walked down the aisle I remember feeling happier than I had ever felt in my life. I folded my hands together as I had been taught to do for my first Catholic Communion. Then I noticed that others had their palms up and their arms extended. When I was blessed, I assumed that pose and felt for the first time that I had a way to channel my devotion and receive God.

It is interesting that, many years later when I told this story to Asha, she said, "I remember." For as long as my family has attended the Palo Alto Temple, Asha has been a Lightbearer there. "I don't know if it was that day, or soon after, but I remember you at that age and the look in your eyes when you would come up for the blessing. The soul is ageless, of course, but most children don't connect as deeply as you did. I've kept my eye on you ever since, praying that you could fulfill in your adult life the spiritual promise I saw when you were nine."

My mother had given me a book called *Sixty Saints for Girls*. I especially liked St. Catherine of Siena because we share the same name. She had her first vision of Jesus when she was just five or six years old. I read and reread that book. I loved the heroism of the saints, and the way so many had to fight for their beliefs and the right to live as they felt guided by God.

I knew Master was my Guru and Ananda was my home. But when I entered my teen years, and was able go out on my own and exert my own will, I became stubbornly determined to go in exactly the opposite direction from those saints I admired. To this day, I don't know why. Apparently there was some karma that had to be worked out.

I always kept Master's picture with me, even as I partied, had boyfriends, and worked hard to be a success in the world. I went to college, but when there was some mix-up with my credits and I wasn't able to finish on time, I quit one class short of graduation.

Still, I was able to land a series of pretty good jobs, and to excel at all of them. My bosses liked me and rewarded me with responsibility and opportunity. Nonetheless, happiness eluded me. Nothing brought the satisfaction I hoped for.

When the contradiction between my inner longing and my outer life was more than I could bear, I abused both food and alcohol. By the grace of God I never did anything terrible or got addicted to anything unwholesome. I played the game of worldly success as well as I could, but it became increasingly more difficult to hide my unhappiness.

Finally, I was so depressed that I couldn't get out of bed for three days. Over and over I prayed to Master, "You have to help me." Lying in bed for those three days, I finally and fully surrendered.

My coworkers, alarmed when I didn't show up, called my parents, and they came immediately to where I was living.

In the past I had rejected all attempts on their part to help me straighten out my life. This time I accepted and went home with them. I left behind pretty much everything, except my dog, my clothes, and my pictures of Master. Home also meant Ananda.

My parents are also committed to Master; and through these years, whenever I came to see them, we would go to Sunday service together.

Asha always expressed warm interest in how my life was going—now I understand why. Sometimes she would mention Ananda Village. "I think you would like it," she would say. But in all those years I could never see myself there.

So I moved in with my parents, and started doing yoga and taking classes at Ananda. Trying to find my way.

Shortly after I returned home, we were at the temple and I happened to see a flyer about a summer program at Ananda Village called *Living with Spirit*. It was for people "under thirty." At that time I had no Ananda friends of my own. I just knew the people my parents knew, who were mostly their demographic, not mine. *Living with Spirit* started in two weeks, and when the day came I was there. I met young people like me who had felt the call of God—and responded. I had found my family.

My mother was determined that I should finish college. Even if I never used the degree, she insisted, it wasn't good for me to quit, especially when I was so close to graduating.

When we brought Asha into the discussion, she was more interested in getting me back to Ananda Village. But she finally said, "You are only one class short. Your parents have been generous and supportive all your life. Even if you don't feel like it, do it for them." Then she added, "Perhaps you can both live at the Village and finish your degree."

I was comfortable in my parents' house, so I started looking into getting that final class done at some college nearby. As it turned out, the one class I needed to get my degree was only offered at one school in all of Northern California. That school was in Sacramento: too far from my parents' house to commute to, but quite doable from Ananda Village.

So I moved to the Village, took the class, got my degree, and, twenty years after I met my Guru, came home to him.

—*from Cate Taylor*

TWICE BLESSED

My uncle did not have a happy life. He was highly intelligent and sincerely interested in spiritual development. But he'd had a brutal upbringing, which he tried to compensate for with drugs and alcohol.

I didn't know him well, so I can't speak of whether the good and harm he did in this world balanced out in the end. But I do know of one good deed for which I am eternally indebted to him.

One morning in meditation, he said, he felt a "nudge from Spirit" to send me *Autobiography of a Yogi* by Paramhansa Yogananda.

I started reading it as I was hiking up a mountainside. By the time I came down, my whole worldview had changed. Before, nothing in life had made sense. Now I knew my purpose was to seek God, and that God was seeking me. I vowed to practice meditation daily.

About six months later, on a Saturday morning, the phone rang in the middle of my meditation. It was my father.

"Your uncle committed suicide," he announced solemnly.

I tried to continue meditating, but the shock was too painful. Overwhelmed by tears and emotion, I decided to journal my experience.

Just after I finished writing, and was wondering how to proceed next through the grieving process, I remembered that I had volunteered to help with a community service project. I decided that keeping the commitment would be an uplifting way to honor my uncle.

The project entailed moving thousands of books from one storage area to another, loading and unloading them from the backs of trucks. I no longer remember whose books they were or why we were moving them.

A couple of hours into it, as I hoisted yet another box up into the back of a truck, one volume slipped off the pile and fell into my arms. It was *Cities of Light* by Swami Kriyananda. I knew that Kriyananda was a disciple of Yogananda, and I felt it was the grace of God that put that book into my hands on that day. When I asked to buy the book, the man in charge gave it to me for free.

Cities of Light is about the ideal of spiritual communities, and Ananda as a living example of that ideal. In the middle of my copy was a card advertising a summer program at Ananda. I mailed it in and a few weeks later received a call.

"Did you know that that card and the book it was in were printed thirty years ago?" the woman from Ananda asked me.

It had never crossed my mind. Of course the program advertised was long over, but another that suited me perfectly was starting in a few weeks.

"Would you like to come?" she asked.

"Yes," I said enthusiastically. My faith was on fire.

As soon as I arrived I felt at home. I don't know if my uncle ever imagined the impact *Autobiography of a Yogi* would have on my life. But perhaps he was helping me all along. I've always thought it significant that, on the day he died, news of Ananda literally fell into my lap from above.

—*from Connor Burke*

RECOMMENDED READING

I was just shy of my twenty-fifth birthday and already I had been through drugs, alcohol, rehab, and the disappointment of a spiritual practice that helped a little, but didn't satisfy my longing for truth.

On a business trip, I stood in front of the Eastern Religions section of the bookstore at the Milwaukee, Wisconsin airport.

"I need a good book," I declared to God, "and I need it now!"

They say that, as you progress along the spiritual path, God first sends you books, then teachings, and finally a guru. To me He gave all three at once. At the time my aspiration didn't reach higher than something good to read. The longing of my heart, though, was greater than my mind knew.

At random I pulled a book off the shelf. It was *Autobiography of a Yogi* by Paramhansa Yogananda. One look into the eyes of the author pictured on the cover and I knew I had found not only a book to read, but a teaching to practice and a master to follow.

Many times since then God has answered my prayers, but never so dramatically and so completely as He did that day.

—from Narayan Romano

Marching Orders

When I met Swami Kriyananda I was powerfully drawn to him and the work he was doing. I had finished college and was living in a cooperative community that a few friends and I had started on a two-hundred-acre farm in Illinois. We had high hopes for what we could accomplish together. Now I felt called to live at Ananda Village in California. Did God want me to leave my friends and all the plans we had made together? Desperately I yearned for clear guidance.

I took my prayers to one of the most inspiring places I knew—a bluff overlooking the Mississippi River, dotted with gnarly red cedar trees. Many of the cedars were hundreds of years old and had grown into exquisite shapes. They looked like carefully cultivated bonsai trees, only full scale. The bluff to me was God's own cathedral, decorated by His hand.

Usually I meditate facing east, but since the question was whether to move west, I sat facing that direction. I was determined to stay there until an answer came.

For many hours I prayed and meditated, but felt no closer to clarity than when I had sat down. Then, all of a sudden, even though I hadn't been singing or thinking of music at all, lyrics to one of Swamiji's songs popped into my head.

> *Some men lack the daring*
> *Ever to be free*
> *They shun the heights*
> *And cloud the depths*
> *And court security*
> *Come, you're a man,*
> *No passive stone,*
> *Stand up and call*
> *Your soul your own*
> *Go on alone,*
> *Go on alone,*
> *Don't look back,*
> *Just go on alone.*

I came down from the bluff and told my friends what I had received. Some wept at the news. We were like a family, and it was hard to think of not being together in this way anymore. But all felt as I did that God was calling me and I had to follow.

I packed my bags and moved to California.

—from Tim Tschantz

NEW WINE

It was because of car trouble that I came to Ananda—my spiritual path and spiritual home.

I was born in Israel, raised by a devout father as a conservative Jew. I loved the Jewish services, ceremonies, and celebrations. But in my teens I began to question the meaning of life and the existence of God. By my late twenties, disappointments in career and relationships had left me empty and dissatisfied.

Lying in bed one night, I shocked myself with a sudden desperate prayer. "*God, show me the way!*" I cried. It was a turning point.

By this time I had moved from Israel to Japan. Now I felt compelled to go to America. I ended up living with a friend in Palo Alto, California.

I had begun to explore Eastern spirituality. Looking through a directory of spiritual groups, I was overwhelmed with choices. How could I know which path was mine? I prayed deeply, "God, You have to guide me."

Soon after, walking down the sidewalk one day, I saw a small sign, "Yoga Center." It was the early days of Ananda Palo Alto, and at that time they had a "storefront church." I went inside to look around. On the altar was a picture of Jesus Christ.

If you aren't Jewish, you may not understand how impossible it was for me to stay in a place where a picture of Jesus was reverentially displayed. I felt like a betrayer. "I AM JEWISH!" I declared to myself, and walked out.

A few days later I had to run some errands, but my car wouldn't start. The battery was dead. I didn't know what to do, so I stood on the sidewalk in front of my house and prayed that someone would help me. A neighbor driving by stopped and asked, "Is there something you need?"

"Yes," I said, "the battery in my car is dead. I need to borrow a car so I can go get a new one."

"Happy to help," she said, and gave me her car to drive.

On the way to the auto shop, I pushed the start button of the cassette player without any idea of what was in there. A woman's voice came on talking about harmony in relationships. Her words touched a responsive chord in my heart. It was Asha, co-director of Ananda Palo Alto.

I started going to Ananda—but only to their library to borrow more tapes. For months I listened to recordings of Asha's classes. There was a deep resonance between what she said and my own inner longing. I began to meditate and, finally, came to a Sunday service. Asha was speaking. Afterwards in the greeting line, when it was my turn, I blurted out, "I am Jewish! I don't know why I am here!"

To my astonishment, pointing to her husband David and herself, Asha said, "We are Jewish, too." Later, Asha reminded me that Jesus had also been Jewish. "He never stopped being a Jew," she said. "His followers called him 'Rabbi.' It was long after he died that Christianity became a separate religion."

Even though I knew Ananda was the answer to my prayer, it wasn't easy to overcome the deep mistrust and many layers of self-identification that caused me to flee that first day. But, through God's grace and my own longing for truth, eventually this Jewish girl embraced not only her Hindu guru, but also Jesus, her Christian/Jewish rabbi as well.

—*from Diksha*

HOMEWARD BOUND

The first time Yogananda gazed into my eyes from the cover of *Autobiography of a Yogi*, I wasn't open enough spiritually even to buy the book and read it. Two years later, in a time of unbearable spiritual darkness and fear, I remembered those eyes and went looking for the book.

I found it in my hometown public library in Louisville, Kentucky. For the next three days I seldom put the book down. Here was the friend I had been seeking in all the wrong places. Alas, he had left this world twenty years earlier. But those eyes assured me that time, space, and death itself could not keep his love from reaching me.

What to do next? I wrote to his organization and waited three agonizing months for a pallid institutional reply, offering me nothing more than I had already. Utterly discouraged, I left Kentucky to live with friends in North Carolina.

On their coffee table, to my surprise, again I saw those eyes looking at me from their copy of *Autobiography of a Yogi*. Next to it was a small book: *The Road Ahead*, by Swami Kriyananda. On the back cover it mentioned Ananda, a community dedicated to Yogananda's teachings.

"I must go there," I decided. I emptied my bank account into my pocket—all of about thirty dollars—and within a week I was hitchhiking to California.

A short way into the journey a fierce migraine headache descended on me. Sitting in the passenger seat of some stranger's car, I could barely distinguish light from dark. My eyes felt anchored to my skull, unable to move left or right. I sank into a torpor of pain.

When the driver let me out somewhere in Boulder, Colorado, I managed to find a small park, and crawled into a shady spot to wait out the pain. I couldn't think or plan beyond that moment. I could barely articulate a prayer for help.

Time was confused, but perhaps it was the next day when I sensed kindly energy around me and vague human shapes and voices. My next memory is lying on a couch in some suburban home, a young couple hovering nearby. The man handed me a fruit drink, and the woman placed her hand on my forehead.

Instantly, the pain vanished, and my vision and mind returned to normal.

"How did you learn to do that?" I asked.

"From Yogananda," she said simply.

I was weak, but functional, so they took me to I-25. The first car that stopped delivered me to my sister's home in Pueblo, where I was able to rest and recuperate before continuing on to Ananda.

I had done my best—and when my best wasn't enough, Master had reached out to me, through his angels, to move me the next step home to him.

—*from Prakash*

BELIEVE

It was pitch black, two hours past midnight, on a deserted country road. A single man (me) was trying to hitch a ride. Not a car in sight. Conditions couldn't have been worse. I lived out in the country where the young people all got around by hitchhiking. But now I was looking at a long, *long*, lonely walk home.

I was raised an atheist, and when I got old enough to think for myself I decided my parents were right. Never one to keep my opinions to myself, I was fiercely outspoken against God and religion.

Yoga, however, interested me. Even meditation. Somehow I practiced both without feeling any contradiction between that and my atheism. Eventually I found *Autobiography of a Yogi*, which soon became a favorite, even though Yogananda spoke a lot about God.

For a long time the atheist in me fought against Yogananda's words, but slowly I began to open up to the world he described. It wasn't easy.

Now, all by myself on that lonely road, I began to sing a song by Yogananda I had recently learned: *O God Beautiful*. Standing under the stars, singing from my heart to God, I hardly recognized myself!

I went on this way for about twenty minutes. Finally a car appeared, but it whizzed by without even slowing down. Then I noticed a distance up the road it had stopped. Nothing like that had ever happened before. Usually either a car stopped or it didn't. I hurried up to it and looked in the window.

There was a woman alone. Another first: Single women never picked up single men. She looked frightened.

Nervously she asked, "Where are you going?" I told her the name of my village.

"I'm going in another direction," she said, "but I'll take you there."

I got in. As we drove away, she said, "I have never picked up a hitchhiker. Not once. I am too afraid. But as I drove past you, I heard a voice say, 'Stop! Take that boy where he is going.' That is the only reason I picked you up."

When I got in the car I still doubted God. By the time I arrived home, I was no longer an atheist.

—from Jayadev

PROBLEM SOLVED

*"Pray this way to God: 'Lord, I will reason,
I will will, I will act, but guide Thou my reason, will,
and activity to the right course in everything.'"*

PARAMHANSA YOGANANDA
~ *The Essence of Self-Realization* ~

Two-Up

After a fire in the kitchen, Earth Song Health Food Store and Café had to close for six months. When we reopened, it was a struggle to win back our clientele and make up for lost sales. I was the manager and regularly put in fourteen-hour days, sleeping several nights a week in the basement "bunk house." It wasn't worth a forty-mile round trip on a winding mountain road just to spend a few hours in my own bed.

It was almost Christmas and we had planned a gala event, hoping to raise our magnetism and end the year on a better financial note. The flyer looked good, and I sent it to be printed two-up on a full-size sheet of paper, then cut in half.

There would be hundreds of cars in town that night for another event, and we planned to leaflet all of them. The print shop was closing for the holidays and all day I kept trying to get over there. Finally, just fifteen minutes before the shop closed, I sent a friend to get the flyers.

Over my desk I had two pictures of my Guru, Paramhansa Yogananda, each, to me, showing a completely different mood. One I called the "Warrior Pose," the other "Compassion." Depending on the task at hand and the need of the moment, I appealed to one or the other for strength and guidance.

My "office" was nothing more than the passageway leading to the public bathroom. There was a doorway to the office, but no door, and therefore no privacy. Even when I was at the end of my rope—as I felt that day—there was no place to hide.

When my friend handed me the flyers, what little rope I had left frayed and snapped. They were printed fine, but they were uncut—two copies side by side on a full-size page instead of the neat, half-page flyers I expected.

How was I supposed to deal with this? The print shop was closed. We had to get out on the street before the cars drove away. Who was going to sit down now and cut apart hundreds of flyers? And how funky would that look if we hand-cut them with scissors?!

I threw the flyers on my desk and myself into my chair and looked from one to the other of my pictures of Master. I couldn't figure out what he wanted from me, or what more I could give him.

In retrospect it is obvious I overreacted. At the time it was the best I could do.

A voice behind me called my name, "Krishnadas?" I whirled around, ready to take out my frustration on whoever had the misfortune to be standing behind me.

It was Cecilia, a former employee, leaning casually against the door jamb. Dangling from her right hand, as if it were her purse, was a huge paper cutter!

"*Why* are you carrying *that*?!" I cried out to her.

Not everyone walks around with a paper cutter; still, my response seemed to her a little exaggerated. "A friend wanted to borrow it . . ." she began.

"Give that to me, I *need* it!" I declared, reaching out and taking it from her.

I looked then at Master, at "Compassion" and the "Warrior." Chastened, I said, "Sir, why do I ever doubt you?"

—from Krishnadas

CHECK!

I suppose I was not the first wife in the history of the world to have no idea what her husband was up to. That was small comfort, however, when out the blue, he asked for a divorce. Of course there was another woman, but he didn't tell me and I didn't find out till some time later.

I was a Rosicrucian at the time. At an evening service in the temple about a month after my husband left, I suddenly got fed up with being sad. "You MUST help me," I prayed. "I don't want to be alone. I don't want my daughter to grow up without a father. You MUST help me."

While I was at it, I added a few conditions. I am Colombian and my husband had been from Mexico; but I said to God, "No more Latinos. My next husband must have white skin and blue eyes—and a good job. I don't want to have to support him. And make him spiritual." God had been important to me ever since I was a child.

After the temple service was a social hour. I was sitting at a table with my cup of coffee when I saw Jay walking in my direction. I'd seen him at the temple before, but didn't know him. *That's the man I'm going to marry*. It wasn't an intention. It was a fact that announced itself from deep inside me.

I guess he must have felt the burst of energy that shot through me at that moment, because he walked right over and said, "May I sit with you?" Since I already knew I was going to marry him, naturally I said yes.

White skin: check. Blue eyes: check.

He reminded me that we had met at a family campout a few years before. He had come with a little girl about the same age as my daughter.

Oops! He's married! I'd forgotten that important detail in my prayer. "God, I need someone who is *available*!"

As it turned out, the child was the daughter of his ex-wife. They had divorced eighteen months before. And he had a good job—check—and admired me for being a businesswoman. At the time I was driving a Cadillac, and he had noticed.

When he found out I was from Colombia, he started talking in broken Spanish, saying he once was fluent but had forgotten a lot of it now. His father had been sent by his company to Colombia, and Jay had spent seven years of his childhood in Bogotá and Cali.

A Spanish-speaking non-Latino who had lived in my own country: CHECK!

Two and a half years later we were married.

—from Amintha Petersen

FALLING RAIN

Maybe it was a mistake to tear the old roof off the church before we got a permit to put on the new one, but it seemed like an okay idea at the time. *A roof and six skylights, and six weeks to get it done before the start of the rainy season—no problem.*

One odd delay after another kept pushing us closer to those pictures of raindrops in the long-range forecast. When we finally had the plans and the engineer's stamp of approval, I took them to the building department, only to hear those dreaded words: "Plan check." That means their engineers would recalculate everything to be sure our engineer got it right.

On a little project like this, though, that process should only take about twenty minutes. "How long before the plans come back?" I asked the man behind the counter.

"Seven to ten days," he replied.

The insulating contractor, roofing guy, skylight installer, and electrician were all poised and ready to go, but we couldn't do anything without the permit. Meanwhile, rain was forecast in five days. The thought of our roofless church soaked by the first rain was not pleasant to contemplate. I called the building department to explain our dilemma.

"I'm the pastor of the Ananda Church and I am in a jam. We tore off the roof and can't put it on again without a permit. Rain is predicted for Saturday. Can you help?"

"Ananda . . ?" the man at the other end of the phone said. "Is that related to Paramhansa Yogananda?"

"Yes. We are his disciples. The church is dedicated to his teachings."

"I read *Autobiography of a Yogi* twenty years ago," the man continued thoughtfully. We talked for a while and then he said, "I'll see what I can do."

At 5:15 that afternoon, fifteen minutes after the department closed, he called back. "Your permit is ready. Come and get it in the morning."

I walked outside the church to thank Master for his timely intervention. Suddenly, on my left, I felt what I can only describe as a *huge* presence, and the feeling of Master's right arm across my back and shoulder, and the gentle grip of his hand. Inwardly, I heard Master say, "Ananda is my work. This is my temple. I've got it covered!"

We finished the roof on Saturday afternoon. That night, as I sat alone in the church preparing for Sunday service, I heard the first rain of the season falling on the new skylights.

—*from Ananta*

HOME SWEET HOME

I moved from California to Italy with two pieces of check-in luggage. Almost everything else I sold or gave away, storing just a few special items for some I-don't-know-when future.

Going from one Ananda community to another, as I was doing, is not the same as landing in a strange place without anyone to help. I was provided a fully furnished place to live—furnished, however, with someone else's possessions. Temporarily, they had no need of them.

The day came, however, when they did need them. Having an uplifting place to live has always been important to me, so it was a good spiritual challenge to be left with nothing but a bed and the two suitcases worth of stuff I had brought from California.

I made a long and detailed list of everything I needed, adding a few non-essentials just because they would be lovely. I listed the prices, totaled the cost, and was not surprised that it was *way* beyond what I could afford.

Then Divine Mother and I had a little discussion. I explained to Her both my finances and my needs. Of course She already knew, but it comforted me to talk to Her about it. Then I folded up the list, put it away, and left it for Her to decide if, when, and how this would work out.

Six months later, everything on that list had been given to me or had come easily at a price I could afford. Even the just-because-they-are-beautiful items came. Plus a washing machine—something so expensive it wasn't even on the list.

The word miracle was never far from my mind as I watched my little home materialize before my eyes—miracle and trust, faith, and gratitude.

—from Uma

AND *the* ANSWER IS...

When I came on the spiritual path I had hit rock bottom. My mind was a mess, the result of a "crisis of faith" during which I had experimented with drugs and alcohol. Add to that a nervous system impaired by difficult surgeries to remove a spinal tumor that had left me paralyzed from the chest down for several years. I was desperate to return to physical and mental health, and to find life's meaning.

At one point in those rocky days I had a dream. I lay on my back at the bottom of a deep well. High above I could see a fragment of the night sky, and in the center, a tiny star. I knew intuitively that if I would faithfully follow the spiritual path I would gradually rise ever closer to the star until its light would fully enfold me. It was a tremendous promise—no matter how far I had fallen, I could be redeemed.

Blind belief, though, wasn't for me. And I was in far too much pain to accept a "pie-in-the-sky-when-we-die" kind of religion. I wanted God's guidance now. And so I read the scriptures and held them to their word, testing them with scientific rigor. Each time I faced a spiritual question, I prayed and demanded an answer. And the answers came.

I was at the beach one afternoon, lying on a towel and reading a spiritual book. I was concerned about my mental balance; and I wondered whether I should consult a Western-style psychologist, or if the path of yoga and meditation would bring the healing I needed.

Following my usual practice of demanding that God answer my question, I put the book down and prayed intently. I sensed that the answer would come if I followed my intuition, which told me to pack up my things and get in the car. Praying continually, I felt guided to drive to the city center.

My favorite bookstore was an enormous place called Warehouse of Books. But my mother had mentioned a smaller bookstore recently, and I felt guided to go there.

When I entered the store, without hesitation I turned to the left, walked three aisles down, turned right, and walked halfway down the aisle, where I stopped and looked at the top shelf to the right. On the shelf was a dusty copy of *Yoga and Western Psychology*, by Geraldine Coster, a disciple of Carl Jung.

I bought the book, and—after driving back to the beach and spreading my towel—immersed myself in its pages, where I found exactly the answers I needed.

—from Rambhakta

A Good Question

My way of leading has always been to give others as much responsibility as they are willing to accept. Still, starting the first Ananda community required that I spend a great deal of time making sure the community developed in a way that would be pleasing to Master.

It was difficult at the beginning, but eventually the community began to thrive and my direct involvement became less necessary. I felt another phase of my life was beginning, when I could do more of the serious writing Master wanted of me, to complete the legacy he had left for me to carry out.

At the same time, the community I had started near Assisi, Italy, was taking hold, and I felt I was more needed there than in America. But I couldn't live right in the center of the community; I would have no privacy and no time to work. Besides, I felt the writing I had to do now required a certain separation, even from the communities I myself had started. Solitude would allow me to think expansively about my Guru's mission. Important though Ananda is, it is only one part of what he gave me to do. I asked Master for guidance.

Soon after, on a visit to Ananda Assisi, I was sitting in the dining room. An Italian woman, to whom I later gave the name "Premi," was sitting across from me. At that time she was quite new. Out of the clear blue sky she said to me, "Why don't you come live here?"

Another woman, Sigrid, from Germany, also new to the community, heard Premi speak. "I feel God wants you to live here," Sigrid said. "If you agree, I will lend you the money to get the place you'll need."

It was the right moment. That very day we found an ideal piece of property. Nearby, but secluded. I still needed money to build a home. Although I have founded communities and written many books, I am not a rich man. I take no salary and no royalties. Whatever has come to me has gone back into developing the work that I do.

It is a policy with me not to go into debt. I never use credit cards unless I can pay them off completely at the end of every month.

In a catalog I found a decent prefabricated house that could be built by volunteer labor at not too high a cost. People pitched in and soon it was ready.

The land I bought with Sigrid's money was more than I needed for myself. Several community members bought portions of it, and in that way we were able to return to her all that she had lent me.

The house in Assisi proved to be just the quiet haven I needed. There I found the inspiration, through God's grace, to continue in the way He guided me in my service to Him.

—from Swami Kriyananda

Fear No More

It started without any warning. First it was just a mild anxiety before I went to sleep. But soon it progressed to a mind-numbing fear that began at dusk and went on for many hours.

Eventually I was diagnosed with Panic Disorder Syndrome, commonly called anxiety attacks. I started taking tranquilizers just to be able to sleep. But soon the pills lost their effectiveness. Sometimes I stayed up most of the night watching movies, just to distract myself from the fear. I tried to analyze the cause (I had been through a long period of overwork), but analysis yielded no relief.

My doctor suggested antidepressants as a long-term solution.

"How long?" I asked.

"For the rest of your life," he said.

I was determined not to go that route. But after nearly five months of nightly attacks that were growing longer and more severe each day, I was running out of options.

Then one day I listened to a recorded talk by Swami Kriyananda called *Spiritual Tests and Right Attitude.* He told a story I'd heard before, but this time it made a deep impression on me.

A secretary of his resigned suddenly in the middle of a crushingly busy period of work. Swamiji had considered her a friend and was hurt that she would walk out on him at such a critical time. Later, during his meditation, he found his mind kept going back to his sense of betrayal. He tried reasoning his way through it, but the feeling was too strong. Reason couldn't overcome it.

"Since I couldn't affirm the negative feeling away," Swamiji said, "I decided to accept it. I went into the core of the feeling and lifted the energy up the spine to the spiritual eye. Then I offered it to God. In that moment the feeling dissolved, and I went on to have a deep and refreshing meditation."

That night, when the usual anxiety struck, I had the most interesting experience. I was terrified, but a part of me was also *bored*.

That was the mental wedge I needed. Instead of edging away from the fear as usual, through drugs or distractions, I decided to try Swamiji's exercise: to accept what was happening and dive into the core of it. I had never tried anything like this before. But I was ready to do something—anything, no matter how terrifying—rather than run away from this feeling again.

As I turned inward to face it, the anxiety was so tangible it seemed to have a mass and shape of its own. I brought my awareness into the center of it. I was surprised to find that it didn't overwhelm me, as I expected it would. I stayed with it as long as I could, until I felt I was really accepting it one hundred percent, without moving away from it even slightly.

With focused awareness I gently lifted that dark mass to the point between the eyebrows. It required extraordinary concentration and will. I was exhausted by the effort.

"I am finished with this," I prayed sincerely. "I return it back to You."

I visualized lifting it out. through my forehead, into the vast infinite.

In that moment the fear simply disappeared. I felt completely refreshed and back to my normal self, as if I had never had anxiety in my life.

I was incredulous.

The freedom, however, was short-lived. Within moments the fear returned, as strong as ever. It took every ounce of my energy to repeat the process again, and then a third time.

After that I sank into a long, peaceful sleep; the first in many months.

Since then I have never experienced another anxiety attack.

—from Karen

DIVINE EFFICIENCY

Probably it wasn't wise for a single woman to set out alone in the middle of a very hot July to drive across the great (big) state of Texas in an old Chevrolet without air conditioning. It was 1978. I was on my way to a new life at Ananda Village in California, and I didn't want to wait another day.

I'd never driven across Texas on my own before. I knew it would be hard, but I felt it was doable. I remembered an old saying my mother told me, which I set to music and sang as I drove and drove. "The sun has riz; the sun has set; and here I is, in Texas yet."

About three quarters of the way across Texas, I began to feel really ill. Maybe it was the heat, or my anxiety about the move, or just the stomach flu, but I started to see white spots before my eyes and felt I couldn't drive any farther.

I checked into a cheap motel somewhere in West Texas, and spent much of an uncomfortable night praying for help. In the morning I felt slightly better, and, more importantly, that God wanted me to go on.

That carried me as far as Las Cruces, New Mexico. But then again I began to feel so ill, I knew if I didn't find help I would have to stop driving. Picking up hitchhikers is not recommended for women driving alone, but I kept thinking, "Perhaps I'll find someone who can drive for me."

Just when I was about to give up completely, I saw two women about my age hitchhiking near a freeway entrance ramp. One was holding a guitar case. As clear as a bell I heard the words, "This is the answer to your prayer."

"Where are you going?" I asked when I pulled up in front of them.

"Sacramento," was the reply. Just a short way from my destination.

"Can either of you drive?" I asked.

"I have a chauffeur's license," one replied, and promptly pulled it out to show me.

"Please get in. Would you drive for me? I'm not feeling well."

As we pulled back onto the highway one of them said, "We were praying that someone kind and safe would give us a ride. We were in a pickup truck with this man but we felt he was not a good person. We made him stop and let us out here. Fortunately he agreed. We were quite scared and felt we needed divine help to go on."

We started talking. They told me their story; I shared mine. They played music for me, fed me soup, and put cold, damp towels on my aching brow. We ended up driving straight through to Sacramento.

We exchanged names and addresses but I never heard from them. I don't think they were angels, but certainly they were angelic in the way they cared for me. I was the answer to their prayer, and they were the answer to mine.

—*from Savitri*

GOOD CAR-MA

A car is something that takes me from here to there. That's everything I know about cars. So twice, when I had to buy one, I wisely turned the project over to God.

The first time I had just moved to Palo Alto, California. You can't live in California without a car, so ignorant or not, I had to plunge ahead.

I found a free newspaper that included a listing of cars for sale. One blurb seemed to jump out at me, saying, "This car is for you!" When I called the owner, he told me he was a devout Christian. What that had to do with his car, I don't remember; but for me it clinched the deal. He believed in God; I believed in God. Without further investigation I bought the car. It served me well for many years.

Eventually, circumstances changed. I didn't need that car as much and couldn't afford to keep it. I was no better at selling a car than I was at buying one. The car had come from Palo Alto, so that seemed the right place to sell it, even though I now lived two hundred miles away.

When I got to Palo Alto, I drove the car to Stanford University and found a bulletin board where I posted a handwritten note about the car. As I turned to walk away, a man tapped me on the shoulder.

"I want to buy your car," he said.

"Do you want to see it first?" I asked. I had bought it sight unseen; I thought other people might shop for cars the same way I did. He took it for a short ride and gave me the money that very afternoon.

Three years later circumstances had changed, and once again I needed a car. I wrote on a piece of paper a few details of what I was looking for: small, efficient, low mileage, color white, and a price I could afford. I put the paper on my meditation altar and asked God to take care of it.

Four months later a friend needed my advice about some major purchases. I was very busy and I'm not fond of shopping, but helping a friend trumped everything so I said yes. In the middle of our shopping trip, I needed to use the bathroom. The nearest one was in a car parts store, a place I would never have entered otherwise.

I saw a free magazine there listing cars for sale. When my hand touched the magazine, I knew it would show me the car I was supposed to buy. I took the magazine home, laid it on the table, and said, "God, You have to guide me." Then I began to turn the pages. Halfway through, there it was: small, practical, low mileage, white, and just what I could afford. I called the owner and immediately liked the sound of his voice.

"I want to buy your car," I said. He lived six hours away, so I asked him to hold the car until I could get there. To prove my commitment I sent him a few hundred dollars.

Soon after, a friend took me to pick up the car. She couldn't believe I was buying a car sight unseen! But I was certain. The car turned out to be in mint condition. The owner was a mechanic! I drove it for seven years and it never gave me a single problem.

The next car was an outright gift from a generous friend. By that time I was married. My husband's contribution was to name the car *Lakshmi*, which means goddess of prosperity. *Lakshmi* is still with us and working fine, so, for now, that's the end of the story.

—from Diksha

The Ten-Percent
Solution

When I had the red carpet laid throughout the house, I thought we'd live there the rest of our lives. "Resale value" never occurred to me. Three years later, to my astonishment and dismay, we were getting a divorce. My husband wanted to dissolve everything, divide it in half, and start over. So my lovely home went on the market.

My second daughter was still in college. Her father felt she was old enough to take care of herself; I wanted to help her finish school. I figured it all out to the penny, including how much I *had* to get for the house.

"Not a chance," the realtor said, "especially with that red carpet."

"Someone will come along who loves that carpet as much as I do, and will pay what we are asking," I told him. I was so confident that I put what was now my half of the monthly mortgage onto my credit card. I had no other way to pay it, but I would never have accumulated such a debt if I hadn't had faith that God would provide.

And He did. The first person that came to see the house, in the first week it was for sale, loved the carpet and bought the house for the price I needed.

My daughter and I got a small apartment near her college, but no matter how many times I added up the figures, I was still short one hundred dollars a month (which was a lot more money in those days). I had reached the top of my pay scale at work, so there was no hope of a raise there.

For years I had tithed ten percent to my church, and for the first time it crossed my mind, "Maybe I can't afford to tithe."

Remembering the realtor and how my faith had proved true, I answered myself emphatically, "You can't afford *not* to tithe." Addressing God, I said, "You are just going to have to help me."

The next month the pay scale at work was changed and I got a fifty dollar raise. The month after that we got another fifty dollar cost-of-living increase.

I've never worried about or been short of money since.

All my life I've had a close relationship with God. I talk to Him about everything. When my husband left, my world shattered into tiny pieces. I was forced to turn to God in a way I didn't know was possible. What I had thought of as a close relationship reached depths of understanding I didn't know were there.

At the time of the divorce I suffered intensely. "What happens to us in life," Sister Gyanamata (an advanced disciple of Paramhansa Yogananda) counseled, "doesn't matter. All that matters is what we become through what we experience." Looked at in this way, I can only think of the divorce as a blessing from God—perhaps the greatest spiritual blessing I have ever received.

—from Gloria

RIGHT TIME, RIGHT PRAYER

Going on a lecture tour was not in itself a daunting prospect. Words come easily to me and I feel it is both my duty and my joy to share with others all that Swami Kriyananda has so patiently shared with me.

Organizing the proposed tour, however, proved to be more than I could do. I had the skill, but not the time. I prayed to Master for help.

That night, the face of my friend Karen appeared to me in a dream. When I awoke I felt God was telling me, "She can help you."

The next day there was a gathering at Swamiji's house. When I saw Karen, I told her about my dream and what I felt from it.

"For a long time I have wanted to work closely with Swamiji, the way you have been able to do," Karen replied. "Often and sincerely I asked God to give me that opportunity. But a year has passed and my prayer has not been answered. Last night it occurred to me that maybe I was asking God to give me something that was not rightfully mine.

"You are close to Swamiji and doing good work sharing his teachings with the public. So last night I prayed, 'If I can't work with Swamiji, perhaps I could work with Asha.'"

Organizing that tour was the first of many projects we have done together in the twenty-five years since the night our prayers intersected. Projects that include helping to edit the book you are now reading.

—from Asha

SHE KNOWS

The transfer from Ananda Village in Northern California to Ananda in Seattle came suddenly. I had four days to find a place for my family to live and schools for two of our three children.

I did as much research as possible. This was pre-internet. Still, with calling friends and looking things up at the library, I was overwhelmed with choices and more than a little stressed. I needed to make a lot of decisions in a very short time.

I spent two days driving all over Seattle getting nowhere. My anxiety increased. Half my time was gone and I still had no idea what to do.

Then a thought occurred to me: Divine Mother would not have sent me to Seattle on such short notice if there were no place for our family to live. In other words, *She must already know* what house was meant to be ours. Instantly, my anxiety evaporated. The whirling constellation of thoughts by which I had hoped to *reason* my way to a solution was replaced by an inward assurance that Divine Mother had a house waiting for me. All I had to do was find it.

Nothing had changed except my perspective. What had seemed an uncertain quest had now become like a children's treasure hunt. The treasure was there. All I had to do was find the clues that led to it.

I looked with new eyes at the well-folded map I had been using for days. I felt I should go to the northwest section of the city.

Once there, I meandered around for a bit, trying to find my next clue. I saw a sign pointing the way to a library and felt I should follow it. As it turned out, I headed in the wrong direction, and was soon completely lost. I was about to stop to check the map when I saw the sign "Library" again.

It pointed to a much larger building than I expected, but trustingly I pulled into the parking lot. It turned out to be a high school. As I gazed at the building, suddenly I realized, "This is my daughter's school! That means the house we are meant to have must be close by." This was fun!

As I drove away from the school I thought, "So far so good, Divine Mother. Where is the next clue?" A moment later I saw a convenience store and remembered the weekly *Home Finder* periodical. I had used it a couple of times in the last two days, but every house I'd called was already rented. But here the *Home Finder* had just been delivered. The plastic band was still around the stack.

Scanning the listings, I found a house that seemed just right and it was only a few blocks away. I felt such joy in Divine Mother's presence that I wanted to stop everything and meditate.

I called the rental agent. "Someone else called before you," the agent said. "He's coming to see the house at 5:00 p.m. You can come then too, but if he wants it, he has the prior claim."

I had the whole afternoon free to explore other options. Given the urgency of my situation, that would have been the logical thing to do. But I felt such profound inner assurance from Divine Mother that I didn't bother.

I arrived at the house promptly at five o'clock. It turned out to be just what I was looking for. Right size, right layout, right neighborhood, and right price. While I was walking around, the other potential renter arrived. The agent left to show him the house. A few minutes later, the other renter and I met in the living room.

After I introduced myself, he said, "Didn't you just give a talk on meditation?" Turns out he had been there. I told him I was moving to Seattle to help lead a meditation center.

"My wife and I also need a place to live," he said, "but this house feels like yours. You take it."

Smiling, I said, "Thank you!" to him and to Divine Mother.

—from Purushottama

PERFECT TIMING

When I finally got a job after a long period of unemployment I was grateful to be working again, so I was surprised when I felt a strong inner call to leave for a month to visit the Ananda community. I had read *The Path*, Swami Kriyananda's autobiography, and I felt God and Gurus calling me from my home in Texas to spend time in California.

I was so certain of my inner guidance that I bought a plane ticket and made reservations to stay at Ananda's retreat—all without telling my boss that he would have to do without me for the month of May. I fully expected when he did find out, I would be out of a job.

Finally I couldn't put it off any longer, and went into his office to tell him. Before I could even open my mouth, my boss said, "I'm sorry, but we are having a slow period, and I'm going to have to lay you off for the entire month of May."

Then he added, "I'm not firing you. I want you back June 1."

—*from Lewis Howard*

BETTER *to* KNOW

My mother's friend wrote with the sad news that five weeks before, her husband had disappeared. He had been depressed for a long time, and she suspected he had committed suicide. He was a doctor. Late one evening he left home to pick up something from his medical clinic, and never came back.

This was in Germany when the country was still divided into "East" and "West." The doctor's car was found on the edge of a large wooded area, not far from the border. After a long but fruitless search, the police became convinced that he had walked into the other Germany.

My mother's friend felt her husband was dead. Since they hadn't found his body, she and her three children were caught in a complicated legal limbo.

My mother felt a strong urge to search the area herself. From the police, she learned where the car had been abandoned, and started searching from that point. The wooded area was five kilometers long. She and my father prayed deeply for divine assistance and felt guided to go into a particularly dense part. An hour later, they found his body.

At first the police were deeply suspicious. Perhaps my parents were returning to the scene of a crime they themselves had committed. My father told the police about their prayer and the guidance they felt. Finally the police realized that even with their search dogs and a hundred policemen, they hadn't gone into that part of the woods.

Not all prayers are answered in a happy way. Even though the ending was sad, the wife was grateful to know where and how her husband's life had ended.

—from Mayadevi

HOMECOMING

When I went to live in the Ananda Community near Assisi, Italy, I fell in love with the city of St. Francis, and everything else about that country. No matter how Italian I felt in my heart, my American tourist visa still ran out every three months and I couldn't stay permanently.

My maternal grandparents came from Italy [see "Grandpa and the Lady"] and immigrants, I learned, had protected the right of their progeny to return to the "home country" if ever they chose to do so. Because of my grandfather, I might qualify for *Recognition of Italian Citizenship*.

I went to New York, where I was born and raised, to gather the long list of required documents. Right away I ran into a glitch.

My grandmother lived in an entirely Italian world. Her babies were born at home. Afterwards, a birth certificate was obtained from the City of New York. My mother's birth certificate was filled out by American authorities who completely misunderstood my grandmother. She, being illiterate, had no idea a mistake had been made.

My mother's name is "Carmello," but it was written down with two more syllables and spelled with a "K." The surname was equally garbled.

My mother's birth certificate was for a person who never existed, and there was no certificate for my mother as she was. Everything that happened afterwards in her childhood was in an Italian-speaking world, and when she became an adult, she spoke English. So that erroneous name never appeared again.

This was critical because it was through her that the link was formed to my grandfather. My mother had died years before, so she couldn't straighten it out herself. The New York State Department of Records told me I could go to court and legally change her name to match her parents, but that would take years and cost thousands of dollars.

I was bewildered. Ananda Assisi felt like my spiritual home. My desire to live there was no mere whim; it was God-inspired. Why would He give me that desire then make it impossible to fulfill? Still, if this were His will, I prayed for the detachment to accept it—addressing my prayer to my Guru, and also to my grandfather, since it was because of him that this was possible at all.

I awoke suddenly in the middle of the night when an inner voice of divine power declared, "Don't give up!" Suddenly, I was flooded with ideas of how to get around this difficulty.

It took many weeks and several trips between my home in California, New York City, and Florida (where my father was living), to accumulate everything I needed. My father had held my mother's birth certificate since the day they were married. Whatever name was written on it, he could swear it was hers. Many of the documents had been originally drawn up in Italian. Each had to be officially translated and marked with a seal. I had to find baptism and communion records in churches that had long since closed or relocated.

No matter what difficulties I encountered, I never lost focus or faith. Negative thoughts found no home in me. Even people who love me would not describe me as a confident, powerful person; but from the moment that voice woke me in the night, I was a version of myself I had never seen before. The command "Don't give up!" activated within me a force that would not be stopped. Whenever one door closed, immediately I found another door to open.

One Friday afternoon at the New York Department of Records I was told that the only official who could give me the signature I needed had already left for the weekend. I was flying back to California the next day and nothing could be done until this signature was obtained, which meant yet one more trip across country.

As I walked out of the building, I remembered that the clerk had said the official worked "upstairs." I went back to the lobby and studied the list of offices by the elevator. I didn't know the man's name or where he worked. "Third floor" seemed like the right one, so I went there. Faced with a long hall and many choices, I went from office to office trying to sense where I would find him. Finally, one office felt right. I explained to the person behind the desk why I was there. He took the paper and signed it. God had led me right to him.

I had been told that the Italian Consulate was very particular, so when I turned in all the papers, it was encouraging to hear the officer say, "This is very well-documented." Six months later I received my Italian passport.

—from Mary Mintey

HOUSE PLANS

I started drawing house plans when I was nine or ten years old. As soon as I finished one set, I would start another. By the time I was seventeen, I had a whole stack of plans for houses I could build, someday, if I had the money.

Years passed. I ended up raising a son, working full time, and going to school. By the time my son went to college, I had my graduate degree. The idea of having my own house returned in full strength.

There was still his college to pay for though. I had a little savings, yet nowhere near what I'd need for a down payment. But I felt God guiding me to buy a home, so I began looking. Within a few days I found just the right one: a simple two-bedroom cottage, seven minutes from where I work.

That evening I went back and sat on the porch of the house, just listening to the wind in the trees. I felt explicit inner instructions to submit a bid for the house. I didn't know where the money would come from, I just knew I had to master my fear and go forward with faith.

The owner accepted my bid, and I had to give him $5,000—money I would lose if later I backed out. I had no idea where the down payment would come from.

Three days before the deadline to sign the papers and turn over a lot of money I still didn't have, a long-time colleague called. Some twenty years earlier, several of us had gone in on an investment. I had put in $9,000 from a small inheritance. As far as I knew, nothing had come of it.

"We have an unexpected buyer," my colleague told me, "for your share of the investment."

I expressed mild interest.

"You don't understand," he said. "Your share is now worth $42,000."

Of course I said yes, bought the house, and lived happily in it for fifteen years. Then I sold it and, with the proceeds, moved to a rural area and built a house of my own design.

—from Terry Strom

ABOVE *the* CLOUDS

The weather report late Thursday afternoon said that the biggest storm in fifty years was going to hit Northern California right where we lived. We had to be in Los Angeles by early afternoon the next day for a big retreat my husband and I were leading. The closest airport was two hours from our mountain home, and we had booked a flight for 9:30 a.m. on Friday.

If the weatherman was right, flights would be canceled. We could leave that night, drive the ten hours, and arrive exhausted, but in time. We didn't know what to do, so we followed a tried-and-true principle: When in doubt, meditate.

At the best of times I can be anxious about flying, so the prospect of going through a storm had my emotions all stirred up. I wanted to drive to our destination and was certain God and Guru would agree with me. I put the question to Master at the start of my meditation, "Do we drive or fly?" I then did my best to put it out of my mind so that I could concentrate on my practices.

About forty minutes later—calmer now, but still inclined to drive—I revisited the question. "FLY!" was the unmistakable answer. I checked again. "FLY!"

My husband was also inclined to drive, and was surprised when I told him the unequivocal answer I had received.

"What time should we fly?" he asked.

"The guidance wasn't that specific," I replied. The weather report said that the storm would get stronger as the day went on, so we decided to try for an earlier flight. Usually it costs a lot to change.

"If this is God's will," I thought, hoping to confirm that we were making the right decision, "we'll be able to switch without extra charges."

I picked the earliest possible departure time, 6:00 a.m., and explained to the lady on the phone why we needed to switch. She decided to waive the usual fee.

We had to leave home at 2:30 a.m. to get to the airport in time. By then the storm had hit, and we drove in heavy rain and high winds. The flight was still on, although when we boarded the plane it was swaying in the wind.

"It will be very bumpy all the way to Los Angeles," the attendant told us. The flight wasn't full, so she added, "Take the seats closest to the wings. That's the safest place on the plane."

My heart speeded up and I started shaking uncontrollably. I concentrated on breathing as deeply and as slowly as I could, praying to God and Guru, "You told us to fly. Now You have to take care of us." I couldn't even speak to my husband, but sat silently, focused on *titiksha*: calm detachment.

"Even at our cruising altitude of thirty thousand feet," the pilot announced over the loudspeaker, "it will be a bumpy ride through strong winds. Stay in your seats with your seatbelts fastened. This includes flight attendants. There will be no drinks or snacks served."

We took off through rain, wind, and hail, the plane swerving left and right as we sped down the runway.

I reminded Master again that we were on this plane because of *his* instructions. As we got airborne, I suddenly heard in my mind lines from the Festival of Light, the ritual we do every week at the Ananda Sunday service. A little bird, representing the devotee on his spiritual quest, is buffeted by the winds of trials and difficulties.

"Give yourself into my hands!" cried the wind. "To your strength I can then add my own."

Then came more remembered words of reassurance, this time from Master's early writings:

Know that you are safe behind the battlements of God's eternal safety, even though death knocks at your door or you are rocked on the seas of suffering.

Ten minutes later, the weather changed completely. No more wind, rain, or turmoil. The flight was smooth as silk. God's peace filled me as tears of relief and gratitude ran down my cheeks. Then came more lines from the Festival:

At last, the little bird heeded [the wind's] counsel. Suddenly it found itself soaring joyously, high above the clouds!

All later flights from Sacramento were canceled. The highway was closed due to flooding. If we had tried to drive, we wouldn't have gotten through.

In Los Angeles it was warm and sunny. The retreat went great. The topic: *How to Know and Trust Your Inner Guidance.*

—*from Diksha*

Go Green

When my relationship of many years ended, I lost not only my boyfriend but also my mechanic. When I needed a new car, for the first time I was all on my own. I could only afford a used economy car, but how to tell a good one from a clunker?

After visiting a few car lots I was more confused than ever.

"Lord," I prayed, "I may be a mechanical idiot but You are not. You have to help me find a reliable, affordable car." A sense of peace settled over me, and in that moment I caught an inner glimpse of a small green car with a wind foil on the back.

A few days later I decided it was time for God and me to go car shopping. I test-drove a few cars, but even with God as my co-driver, I felt as confused as ever. Then, on the far side of the lot, I saw a green car with a wind foil.

"What is that?" I said, pointing excitedly toward it.

"I can give you a really good price on that one," the salesman assured me.

I ran over and purchased it on the spot. The salesman was amazed at my sudden transformation from confused and indecisive to knowing exactly what I wanted!

A few hours after I bought the car, it occurred to me that a little "due diligence" might be in order. I looked up the make and model in *Consumer Reports*.

It had mediocre marks in *every* category and was definitely *not* a "Recommended Purchase."

"You led me to this car," I said to God. "You helped me pick it out. It is my car now, come what may."

That little green car ran perfectly without needing a single repair for one hundred and fifty thousand miles.

—*from Lynn Lloyd*

YOU HAVE MAIL

Moving out of the house that she and my father had built together—the place we had called home for forty-five years—was not an easy transition for my mother.

It took over a month to divide a lifetime of memories into "Keep" or "Give Away." The new condo would only hold a fraction of what she had accumulated.

For weeks the old house was in shambles with boxes, packing materials, and stuff everywhere. Each time we took a box to the condo, we carefully unpacked and put everything away. Mom was already living there, and we wanted her to feel comfortable and at home.

A few days after she moved to the new place, Mom realized she had lost the keys to the doors and the mailbox. Using the garage door opener she could still get in and out, but mail was piling up and there was no way to retrieve it. It was disconcerting for Mom to start her new life in such an inauspicious way.

"I am sure the keys are at the bottom of a box or buried under packing material," I assured her. "They'll turn up."

But when everything had been moved, unpacked, and put away in the condo, and every nook and cranny of the old house had been emptied and cleaned, the keys were still nowhere to be found. Mom gave up and called the locksmith. She gasped at the $400 price tag for changing the locks, but she had no choice and set up an appointment for the next morning.

At 3:30 a.m. on the day the locks were to be changed, I woke from a dead sleep. Although I was fully alert, I didn't open my eyes because of the interesting picture unfolding in the darkness before my closed eyes.

First I saw a coat my mother often wore. Then, in our downstairs closet, I saw the coat hanging. In one pocket I saw the door keys for the new condo; in the other pocket, the keys to the mailbox. "How odd," I thought as I went back to sleep.

A few hours later, when I woke again, I remembered what I had seen and immediately went to the closet. The coat was hanging just where I'd seen it, and in each pocket were the missing keys! My mother sometimes takes care of our daughter. I presume she wore the coat over one day and left without it. In the chaos of moving she hadn't noticed it was gone.

When I called my mother she was surprisingly matter-of-fact. "Thank God," she said. Then, referring to the patron saint of lost things and missing persons, she added, "All night I have been praying to St. Anthony."

—from Kyle McDonald

Go!

The phone rang, more than once, but I saw no reason to interrupt my meditation to answer it. I was living at Mt. Washington, headquarters for Self-Realization Fellowship in Los Angeles. My room had a small basement and I had turned that space into a meditation "cave."

I was responsible for our meditation groups and in that capacity was scheduled to fly to Oakland to meet with leaders and members there. I knew who was calling. It was Bernard Tesiere, who was to accompany me to the plane, but I checked my watch and saw that I still had plenty of time.

A short time later, my meditation was again disturbed, now by urgent knocking at the door of my room. "Why are they so impatient?" I thought. This time, I switched on the light before looking at my watch. It was a whole hour later than I thought! My wrist had been turned at an angle and I hadn't read the watch correctly! If I missed the plane my entire program would be interrupted.

Quickly as possible, I gathered my things, and a few other friends to help, and we rushed to the car. I did the driving. As I speeded along, one friend watched out the back for police cars, the other looked out the front. We all prayed urgently to Master for help, that I make the plane and not be stopped for speeding.

There were about seventeen stoplights along the way. All were green! When I reached the check-in counter I asked the woman there to call the gate and if possible hold the plane. As I ran across the lobby, I reached into my pocket for the ticket. Some loose change came out with it and fell onto the floor, but I couldn't even stop to pick it up.

They did hold the plane. So I made it in time.

—from Swami Kriyananda

GR 8

I am as fascinated with the placement of numbers as I am with the letters of the alphabet. When I changed residences a few years back, I needed a new phone number. So I called AT&T and told the representative that I would like three eights in a row included among the last four digits of my new number. I explained that I'd always had them, and it meant a lot to me to have them again. He was quiet for a few moments as he clicked away at his computer keys, searching.

Finally he told me there were no numbers available like that, and offered several alternatives. None was acceptable. This had taken quite a bit of his time, so I was willing to compromise. "All right, then. What about two eights next to one another, with the other two numbers adding up to eight? I prefer even numbers." After searching again, he suggested, "What about 3588?" "No. That won't do. Three and five are *odd* numbers; as I said, I prefer *even* numbers."

At this point I was afraid he was going to disconnect the call(!), but he gave it one last try. "What about 2886?" I was heartened and replied, "Love it. The two and the six are even numbers, and with one of them on either side of the eights, they embrace them as though they were family. Thank you so much for your time and patience."

We finished the call and, as I hung up the phone, out of curiosity I looked at the telephone keypad to see if 2886 spelled anything. When I "read" 2886 I laughed out loud, looked up to the ceiling, and said aloud to Master, "How EVER did you do that?"

My license plate for twenty-four years has been AUUUUM. One of my websites is www.auuuumm.net. I start every class I teach with a prolonged "AUUUUUUM."

2-8-8-6 spells A-U-U-M.

—from Vimala

HIGHWAY PATROL

I don't take Divine Mother's assistance for granted, but Her record with me on the highway is pretty impressive.

I was with a female friend in San Francisco, on the way to the flower mart to get bouquets for a big event, when—BAM!—a tire blew. Very dramatic. I pulled into a gas station at the same time a man I didn't know pulled up to the pump. He leapt out of his car and rushed over to me.

"I just love to help!" he said. A few minutes later, he had changed the tire and we were back on the road.

Another time I was in the middle of nowhere with a group of friends traveling in a vintage VW camper. Everything in the car worked fine except the gas gauge, so of course we ran out of gas. One of the guys started walking back to an emergency call phone we'd passed; another started hitchhiking toward the next town.

I began to pray. As soon as the guys were out of sight, a big truck with flashing lights pulled in behind us. It was a fireman on his way to an emergency response workshop, and we were like his homework. Naturally he carried an extra can of gas.

So one day when I was driving on a winding mountain road near where I live, and unexpected rocks on the road blew out my tire, I was surprised that a few minutes passed and no one had come to help.

"Divine Mother," I said playfully, "what's taking so long?" At that moment a pickup truck pulled up next to me.

"Sorry you had to wait," the driver said. "I was going the other way and had to make a U-turn. Then I had to get those rocks off the road before I could come and help you."

—from Mantradevi

HAPPILY EVER AFTER

By the time I was thirty, I had already been married and divorced. In the decade after, I married and divorced again, and two other serious relationships started and ended.

You would think at that point I would have given up and become a nun! My spiritual path supported that alternative. But in my heart I knew my desire for a successful marriage was too strong.

Despite all these heartbreaks, I never felt abandoned by God.

At one particularly painful period, I had to attend the wedding of a friend, even though my heart was raw from a recent breakup. At the reception, I huddled alone in a corner of the room, not wanting to spoil the festive occasion with my sad mood.

Swami Kriyananda sought me out. "I had a dream about you last night," he said. "You seemed very sad."

I acknowledged that his dream was true. "This is a hard day for me." I didn't have to explain; he knew why. We talked about superficial things for a few minutes longer before he left to speak with others. No circumstance of my life had changed, but after that brief encounter with Swamiji my heart felt lighter and a glimmer of hope returned.

Later I wondered, "Did he really dream about me? Or was that just his way of saying, 'I know what you are feeling. God knows. He is with you.'"

I married and divorced the first time before I came to the spiritual path. In the throes of that disappointment, I went every day at lunchtime to the roof of the building where I worked so I could be quiet and alone. I hadn't yet learned to meditate, but I knew how to pray.

"God, you *must* help me. I don't know what to do. You *must* help me."

One day I distinctly felt a divine response: "Today your prayer will be answered." When lunch hour ended, with eager anticipation I went back to my desk.

An acquaintance said, "I'm going to Ananda this weekend. Do you want to come along?"

"Yes!" I said, without a moment's hesitation.

In that first weekend at Ananda I knew I had found my spiritual path. Many people seemed anciently familiar—friends, I believe, from past lives who became dear friends also in this incarnation, including the man who became my second husband. He helped me to learn to meditate, to understand Ananda's teachings, and, within a couple of months, to move to the community.

Alas, that marriage, too, ended in divorce, but at the time his help seemed the answer to my prayer. And I believe it was. The marriage did not have a happy ending, for I had many lessons still to learn. But finding my Guru and moving to Ananda were still the happiest beginning and ending I could have imagined for myself.

Yet the relationship issue, all these years later, was still unresolved. I felt I had to get more serious about putting this part of my life in God's hands. I had long known about an affirmation Yogananda had written to help people attract an appropriate life-companion. Through the years

I had made halfhearted attempts to repeat it. Now I put my whole will into it: *"Heavenly Father, bless me that I choose my life companion according to Thy law of perfect soul union."*

The affirmation itself became my life-companion. Every day, as much as I could, I repeated it. A few people told me how well it had worked for them, and how quickly. Their happy relationships were living proof.

Weeks went by, then months; then a year, then two. Despite my loneliness, the affirmation itself gave me hope. I remembered the words of Sri Yukteswar: "Everything in future will improve if you are making a spiritual effort now."

After several years living outside of California, I decided it was time to come home. I tried to find a place to live, and a job in either of the two communities where I'd lived before, but nothing opened up for me. Nothing. The only option was a community I found entirely unattractive. But I had no choice. Every other door was closed.

My sister had suffered several bouts of cancer; and the one advantage of that community was its proximity to her, which proved God-sent. Her cancer did return, and soon after, took her life. Living there I was able to assist more than I could have from anywhere else.

My love for my sister and, I believe, my call for a soul companion, brought me there. Within a month of moving, a friendship started that blossomed into romance, and then became—for twenty years now—the happy marriage I have always longed for.

God answers our prayers . . . eventually.

—*from Anonymous*

MOTHER'S CARE

Moving to Ananda Village bears no resemblance to entering a cloistered monastery. Still, when I made the move, I turned over to God and guru all my worldly responsibilities. Since I was single with no children, it was the care of my mother I was giving to Him. Inwardly I felt Master promise, "I will."

Whenever I visited my mother, I was comforted by a feeling of God's loving presence around her. Once she hosted a large group of us, including Swami Kriyananda, when we were giving a program in the city where she lived.

Swamiji was impressed by her dignity and kindness. She loved him and all my Ananda friends. My mother never embraced our beliefs or lifestyle, but I felt Master's promise to take care of her included this touch of divine awakening.

Later she lent a substantial sum of money to Ananda at a time when it was desperately needed. I was moved by the faith she showed in the life I had chosen.

For many years she lived happily on her own. Eventually, though, age took its toll.

Her physical debilities put her in nursing facilities where almost all the residents had lost both body and mind. Her mind, however, was crystal clear. Two places proved entirely unsuitable. I had hopes for the third, but now the director was telling me it wasn't working out there either.

I live hundreds of miles from my mother and was scheduled to fly home that afternoon. Holding back tears, I asked the director, "Do you know of any place that would work for her?" She gave me a two-page printed list.

I left to buy some food and used the few minutes alone in the car to have a frank conversation with Master.

"How am I supposed to figure this out in the little time I have? I don't even know where to begin?"

I had looked at the list, but line after line of names like "The Torch," "Hillcrest," and "Tall Pines" had left me utterly bewildered as to what to do. I was surprised when I felt Master answer my prayer, saying, "Look again."

In the middle of the second page the name "Four Seasons" jumped out at me, igniting a light in my consciousness. Had I even seen that name before?

I called immediately. It was a private home in a residential area that a couple had converted into a care facility for elders. A beautiful outdoor garden with flowers, fruit trees, and a gazebo was easily accessible to residents via a winding wheelchair walkway.

One room was available. They even let my mother bring her personal furniture, which, of course, was a great comfort to her.

The last year of her life was spent in these pleasant surroundings with loving caregivers.

When I had given my mother's care to Master all those years ago, he promised to look after her. And he did.

—from Maria McSweeney

THE RIGHT FOUNDATION

I always had a pretty fixed idea of what a man was supposed to be. When I grew to be well over six feet tall and entered the construction trade, this nicely supported my ideal of manhood as strong, reliable, honest, and a good provider for his family. As for emotions, my motto was: don't have 'em, don't need 'em.

It worked well for a while. I built a good business, got married, and raised two kids up to high school age; then everything began to change. After eighteen years of marriage, my wife seemed angry all the time. Two years of counseling didn't do much for the marriage, but it opened me up to issues going back to my early childhood that I didn't even know were there.

For the first time in my life, I had to take seriously the emotions that had been roiling around just below the surface for as long as I could remember. Gradually I adopted an entirely new worldview: emotions are okay. Everyone has them, like feet and hands. The job is to learn how to work with them constructively so that they benefit, rather than injure, the people around you.

It was an epiphany. I joined a men's meditation group and entered a period of tremendous personal growth. I had been raised Catholic, but to me it was just dogma. Now I began to understand the reality of a higher power, of God and the role He could play in my life if I surrendered to Him. I began to pay attention to more subtle influences; and I noticed that my strong thoughts often materialized around me.

The marriage couldn't survive the transformation I was going through. My image of what it would mean to fail as a father and husband included me living in a seedy one-room tenement, with blistered paint on the walls and a bare bulb hanging from the ceiling.

When the marriage broke up, my wife and kids stayed in the house which I had to keep supporting. There wasn't much left over for me to live on, so friends offered the use of what they called their "guest house." This turned out to be a room that looked pretty much like what I had pictured in my failed-as-a-husband scenario.

In a way it was a relief. My worst fears had been realized. I didn't have a lot left to lose, and that allowed me to open up to whatever was trying to happen in ways I never could have before.

This was good, because God had more "unthinkables" to give me.

I'd been in the construction trade for thirty years. I ran a really successful company and never had even one dissatisfied customer.

Just at the time my marriage broke up, I got one of the biggest contracts of my career. A developer hired us to do the framing on fifteen custom homes he was building, each worth from three to five million dollars.

Everything started fine, but by the third house I was about $250,000 in the hole. With all the materials I had to buy, my company couldn't carry a deficit like that. I was looking at bankruptcy.

I had bid the job correctly. My carpenters were working well, as they always had; but the subcontractors on the sites before us were doing shoddy work. Having to correct foundations that weren't square and level was eating up all our time and money.

I didn't see how I could finish the project or save my company. Business failure, like divorce, was way outside my concept of being a man.

I asked for a meeting with the developer and his son. The father had put up the money; the son was the on-site manager.

The meeting was set for Saturday morning. I had just started a meditation practice, and I understood that one of my goals was to give everything to God. I had already lost my marriage; now it looked like my business was going too. While meditating before the meeting, I told God that, whatever happened, He and I would just move on together.

The son took over the meeting almost immediately. For most of the next hour he railed against me and the shoddy work he said I had done. There was a lot I could have said about the subcontractors who had done their work before our team did ours, but I felt no need to justify myself to this man. Nor did I want to set up the subcontractors for the same tirade I was receiving. I had given the whole situation to God and I was content to let Him figure it out.

Finally the father made his son stop. And he asked me what I had to say for myself. (After all, I had called the meeting.)

"I'm $250,000 in the hole," I told him. "I am going to have to file for bankruptcy. I've given you the best work I can. That is all I can do."

The father asked his son to step out of the room with him. After a few minutes the father came back alone and handed me a check for $250,000. "We don't want you to go bankrupt," he said. "We enjoy working with you, and we want you to finish this project. We'll pay what's needed to have you do that."

From then on things seemed to go better. Maybe by the fourth house the subcontractors figured out how to build a better foundation. At any rate we finished on time and—including the extra $250,000—within budget.

—from Paul Fochtman

TIME

My husband had a heart attack when our three children were all under the age of six, the youngest just a newborn.

I was working a fifty-hour-a-week job and, in off hours with my co-workers, developing an on-site daycare center. I volunteered with the PTA, which meant more to me than my work. I loved being with my children but I was only occasionally able to spend much time with them.

My husband and I had been partners in childcare and household duties. During the week he did most of the cooking and shopping. Now his only job was to heal. I felt I had to protect him from the stress of caring for the two older children. Bathing, dressing, feeding, playing, bedtime stories, and doctors' appointments all fell on my shoulders. The only thing my husband could do was to hold the baby while I did everything else.

One month later, my father-in-law died. He was integral to our family, and his passing left a huge hole in our hearts and in our lives.

A few months later my mother died under tragic circumstances. She was a great mom to my sisters and me, and as a grandmother my children adored her. My dad had died ten years earlier. Since then she had struggled with loneliness and depression. I despaired that I had not been able to protect her from her inner demons. She lived just a few miles away, and when she passed, yet another gaping hole opened in our lives.

At the best of times I would have staggered under these multiple blows. Now I didn't even have my husband to lean on. He needed all his strength to heal, and I couldn't burden him with my struggles as well.

Finally one Sunday morning at church, I reached my limit. I was so worried about everything that I was hardly sleeping. I didn't know what God could do about this avalanche of troubles, but clearly I couldn't handle it myself. I surrendered completely to Him.

"Please release me from this stress," I prayed. For the next weeks at home, work, and church, that was my constant prayer. "Please release me from this stress."

The solution God found was one I never imagined and would certainly not have chosen myself. I lost my job. I'd been there twelve years, and getting laid off meant the loss (again) of people who were as dear to me as my own relatives. It was traumatic to be severed from something so central to my self-definition.

Immediately, though, it freed up a lot of time! Fifty obligated hours a week, plus after-hours on the daycare project—GONE! The loss of income meant we had to live more simply. But fifty percent of my salary had been spent paying others to look after our children while I worked. Not having that expense, using our savings, and the severance package I got made it not so bad.

Now I could help my husband exercise, cook the foods he needed to heal, assist him in managing his business, spend time with my children, and volunteer even more at their school. For the next five years I was a stay-at-home mom and loved it.

Losing my job was at first so harrowing that it took me awhile to realize it was a masterstroke by God in answer to my prayer. —*from Anonymous*

Stonewalled

We sited the house carefully according to the principles of *Vaastu*, an ancient Indian system for creating harmony between human activity and natural forces. The doorways, windows, and placement of rooms inside had all been carefully worked out. Architectural plans had been drawn up accordingly. Permits had been obtained. Months of work and tens of thousands of dollars of expenses were all coming to a focus now as the bulldozer began to dig out for the foundation.

Harmonizing with Nature is central to our understanding of life. So we had also done ceremonies and prayers to honor and communicate with the devas and nature spirits on our land, telling them our intentions, in the hope that they would welcome and cooperate with our efforts to put our home in the midst of theirs.

There was a small piece of rock sticking out of the ground right in the center of where the house had to sit, but we assumed it would not cause any difficulty. After it was pulled from the ground, we planned to put it in a place of honor elsewhere.

Several hours later the bulldozer had dug four feet down in a circle twenty feet across, revealing that small piece of rock to be a huge granite boulder. Not knowing how much deeper the rock went, or where the edges were, the driver of the bulldozer was increasingly reluctant to continue to dig near it.

"If it hits that granite, my bulldozer blade will shatter into pieces," he said. "It has happened before and I can't afford to risk my expensive machine. We need dynamite." Contractors always "know a guy," and this man was no exception. It turned out that his "dynamite guy" happened to be in the area, and soon the two of them were looking at the rock, planning where to put the blasting caps.

We didn't know what to do. On one hand, the granite rock had to be removed. It was sitting exactly where the house had to go. On the other hand, after all our careful efforts to work in harmony with Nature, to begin our house by blasting to smithereens a piece of granite that had been there much, much longer than any of us had been on the planet did not seem like the kind of harmonious house building we were hoping to achieve.

The workers took a lunch break. We went into the small cabin we lived in on the property and prayed to God, Guru, and the devas in charge of the land—and especially the ones in charge of that rock. We promised "Brother Rock" that if he had to be dynamited, he wouldn't be taken away altogether. We would use the pieces to make stonewalls.

After lunch the driver of the bulldozer continued to level the ground beyond the perimeter of the exposed rock. But he came too close to the four-foot slope he'd dug earlier, and his machine slipped down the incline and the blade hit the stone.

Instead of the blade shattering as the driver had predicted, the granite rock broke into thousands of pieces. Neither the dynamite guy nor the bulldozer man had ever seen or heard of anything like that happening before.

We have many yards of beautiful stonewall now, thanks to the loving self-offering of that big granite boulder.

—from Devadasi & Alex

In Case of Fire

The schoolhouse was well built, but unfinished. Set at the top of a hill overlooking what we euphemistically called "downtown Ananda," the only access was up a poorly maintained, deeply rutted tractor trail.

Not that it mattered to us. We had moved from a converted chicken coop, so this was luxury indeed. There were six children and one teacher: me.

This was 1973. Everything about Ananda Village was primitive in those days. Education for Life as a worldwide movement, the Village as only one of a global network of spiritual communities, nice houses, paved roads—these things didn't even live yet in our imagination. We were a happy group of pioneers, wading through mud in the winter and dust in the summer, living in trailers and teepees and having a fabulous time doing it.

My resume to lead the school was meager: one year of experience in the public school system. But that was enough to convince me there had to be a better way to educate children.

At Ananda Village I found a group of parents who shared my hope, but with no better plan than I had! The seven children who became my school were simply running around the community getting into mischief. Anything was better than that!

Within a year the community had the shell of the schoolhouse ready. The children and I were already having a great time and the new facility just made it better.

One day at recess the children became very excited as they watched a car making its way up the tractor trail. No one had ever attempted to do that before! It turned out to be an official from the Office of the California State Fire Marshal. He was there to inspect the school. We certainly hadn't invited him. Someone must have told him we were there.

I greeted him cordially, but he didn't smile in return. He just gave a perfunctory greeting, pulled out his clipboard, and began walking around the building taking official-looking notes.

Finally he spoke. "There has to be a way for a fire truck to get in here in case of emergency. You need to put in a paved road to connect the schoolhouse to the public road."

I was in shock. The public road was a mile away.

"How much do you think that will cost?" I stammered.

"About $500,000," he said. "I'll be back in three weeks and I expect to see substantial progress by then." As he turned to leave he added, "Or else I'll shut down the school."

I operated the school on $50 a month, and that included my salary. No, that's not a misprint; I haven't left off any zeros. Everything at Ananda at that time was done on a shoestring—not even the shoestring of a man's work boot, but the shoestring of a child's sneaker. That inspector might as well have asked me to pay off the national debt.

"Well, Master," I said, speaking inwardly to my Guru, Paramhansa Yogananda, "obviously, you are going to have to take care of this. There is nothing I can do."

Then to myself I said, "No point in wasting energy worrying about it." About three weeks later the children were again excited to see a car struggling up the tractor trail. Reluctantly I went out to face what I assumed would be the promised return visit from the inspector. Was this going to be our last day of school?

A different man, with a much friendlier expression, emerged from the car. The other guy, he explained, had decided to switch to the Arson Inspection Division. I made no comment, but thought to myself, "Tracking down arsonists would suit him just fine."

As the new man walked around the building, I waited nervously for him to ask about the paved road.

"The issue here is fire safety," he said finally. "We don't want the children to get trapped in a burning building." I nodded in agreement, but said nothing.

Looking around with a pleased smile on his face, the inspector said, "But there is a lot of open space around the schoolhouse, so I don't think that would be much of a problem. What you need is a good warning system."

"Yes," I said rather tentatively, expecting the next request to be an expensive sprinkler system.

"I was thinking," the inspector continued, "that a good whistle would do the trick. Something really loud!"

"A *whistle*?!" I repeated. Then quickly added, "Yes, sir. A fine idea. A whistle. We can do that!"

He handed me a paper to sign. "This is your promise," he said as I wrote my name in the space he indicated, "that you'll take care of the situation."

Mentally I made a note to set aside $1.25 from the monthly budget to comply with the California State Fire Marshal's request.

For the rest of the year I faithfully wore that whistle around my neck whenever school was in session.

—*from Michael Nitaix*

HEALING PRESENCE

❧

"And the voice of the Lord answered,
'Where My light is,
there no darkness can dwell.'"

PARAMHANSA YOGANANDA
~ The Essence of Self-Realization ~

BREATHE EASY

My daughter was three years old when the doctor told me I only had a few months to live. My symptoms had been concerning—difficulty breathing, extreme tightness in my chest. That's why I went to the doctor. But never in my wildest imaginings did I expect the diagnosis I received.

Fibrosis of the lungs—sometimes it develops slowly; but it can also, as in my case, come on fast and furious.

I was living in America; my parents were thousands of miles away in India. I had nowhere to turn. In a state of helpless, uncomprehending grief I collapsed on my bed.

My mother had given me a copy of *Autobiography of a Yogi*. Now it was sitting on my bedside table. I picked up the book and placed it on my chest as a way to be closer to God and also to my mother.

I have no clear memory of the next three days, which I spent mostly in bed with the book on my chest, crying to God for help. Somewhere in my shock and delirium the image came to my mind of my lungs growing into a large, open hole. Then the gurus—Yogananda and all the others to whom I had ever prayed—one by one entered this opening and began to sweep the fibrosis out of my lungs.

Eventually I began to feel better. *Much* better. I got up from bed and went back to the doctor. Only a few days had passed since he had pronounced my case hopeless. The doctor was astonished. The only word he could use was "miracle." The disease was gone.

That was three years ago. The only treatment I have taken since is to practice breathing exercises. I am hale and hearty, without a trace of the fibrosis that at one time threatened to leave my young daughter without a mother.

—from Anonymous

GOOD MEDICINE

It was a serious illness and the only thing the specialist could offer me was a risky treatment with severe side effects. Naturally, I hesitated, and so did the doctor. But after three years with no significant improvement, even those side effects began to look like the lesser of two evils.

I was back at the hospital. Things weren't looking good, but still the doctor hesitated. He left the room to look once again at the x-rays, promising when he returned to give me a definite answer one way or another.

Knowing that my fate was on the line, I prayed intensely for guidance.

A few minutes later the doctor returned. For three years he had been wavering. Now he spoke with absolute conviction, "Do not take this treatment. Definitely not."

A few months later, without any further treatment, my health began to improve.

—from Bharat

DIVINE THERAPY

I had been a speech therapist for many years, but this was the first time I had worked in a nursing home with so many frail elders. In that setting the therapy I offered was mostly about swallowing, not speech. People who don't work with that population may not realize how serious it can be for an elder person not to swallow properly. Food and liquid get aspirated into the lungs, which can have dire, even fatal consequences. The gurgling sound the breath makes that people call the "death rattle" is because of fluid in the lungs. A person literally drowns to death.

One of my clients was in very bad shape. He had a medical condition that caused him to have repeated strokes. He would make a little bit of progress in learning to swallow properly, then stroke again and be right back where he started. Several times after a positive session in the afternoon, the next morning his breath would again be gurgling in his lungs.

Since conventional therapy was not getting us anywhere, I thought I would try healing prayer. At Ananda I had learned to pray with upraised hands, chanting AUM out loud to "permeate the ether" with my prayer requests. In the nursing home, with the halls full of medical personnel and the doors of the rooms kept open, I thought I should do something less obtrusive.

The man was sitting in a wheelchair and I stood behind him. I prayed to Master to use me as his instrument. Then, mentally chanting AUM, I placed my hands gently on his shoulders.

I was somewhat new to the practice of praying for people, and certainly didn't think of myself as a healer, so I didn't know what to expect. I pictured healing energy flowing through my hands into his body. At first, I just visualized it. Then, suddenly, an actual force began to move through me. I was awed, even a little stunned, by its power. It went on this way for some time. Afterwards, I felt that was enough therapy for one day and I left him to rest.

Somehow I thought he might have died during the night. I certainly expected to hear his breath gurgling the way it had most mornings since I started working with him. To my surprise I found him breathing normally. He was able to do all of the therapy I recommended for him, and at the end even safely take some food and liquid. He stopped having strokes and had no more swallowing or breathing problems.

Since then I have worked with hundreds of elderly people. No one to my experience who aspirated fluid the way this man did ever recovered—no one except him.

He was still frail, but he was pulled back from the brink of death and became a longtime, relatively healthy resident of that facility.

For a while I was concerned that I had done something wrong in healing him, given the confined conditions in which he had to live. Soon I realized I was taking too much credit to myself.

I was not the *source* of the healing energy that flowed through me. God had inspired me to pray for that man, and it was His energy that healed him. It was that man's karma to live longer, and perhaps, I pray, make more spiritual progress before he passed away.

—from Mukti

The Comforter

My parents were fundamental in their religious beliefs and strict in their parenting. Our church was First Assembly of God. They took us five children to services there at least twice a week. Mother was also a Sunday school teacher, caring and devout, with a loving heart.

About the age of six, I came down with an agonizing flu. Fortunately, it wasn't life-threatening, but I ached with fever, my throat burned, and I could hardly breathe. Mother's distress was as great as mine.

She tried everything to ease my suffering, but to no avail. Finally she said, "Let us pray." Her faith itself was a comfort to me. I was very young and my mind was confused by the fever, so I don't remember what she said.

What I do remember is that instantly the pain stopped and I was healed. "How deeply I am loved," I thought, in gratitude and amazement, "not only by my mother, but also by God."

—from Amara

KITTY BLISS

My husband and I moved into a house where two cats were part of the bargain. I love cats, but I was allergic to them. Just a few moments in the company of a cat started me sneezing, sniffling, and rubbing my itchy eyes. So we kept them isolated in the laundry room with a cat door that gave easy access to the outside. They seemed fine, but we adored them and would have loved to share the whole house.

Then we got new jobs in a new country and had to leave the house and cats behind. The compound we moved into was overrun with rats and mice. A cat was the obvious solution. A stray kitten was plucked from the street to live in the common kitchen, but he caused problems for the cook.

"Please take that cat away," he said to us.

Naturally, we hesitated; but if we didn't take the kitten, he would be returned to the street, and our tender hearts couldn't accept that.

He proved to be a delightful roommate, with his acrobatic feats and his playful, affectionate nature. We were in a new country, in new jobs, and the kitten was a spot of joy in an otherwise stressful situation.

At first we kept him off the furniture, hoping to minimize my allergic reaction. But his favorite napping spot was in the middle of our bed, and we didn't have the heart to dislodge him.

Curled up beside the kitten one evening I prayed with great intensity, "Dear God, this little creature is such a blessing to my husband and me. *Please take away these allergies!*"

In that moment I felt a change within me. The allergy was gone. I could bury my nose in the kitten's fur without a sneeze, sniffle, or watery eye.

—from Anonymous

PUZZLED

My elderly friend had such severe pain in his legs that he could hardly sit, walk, or even lie down comfortably to sleep. He was such a skeptic that I didn't want to pray for him without his permission.

"Sure," he chuckled when I asked him. "It won't do any harm."

That same night, after my meditation, I asked Divine Mother to ease the pain in his body—and maybe ease his skepticism as well. I left it up to Her and just let the prayer flow from my heart.

The next day I received an email. My friend was astonished. "Amazing" was the only word in the subject line.

"I am without pain for the first time in many weeks," he wrote. "The medieval term would be that you possess the power of a witch. But this is the twenty-first century, and everything must be explained scientifically. Yet I can make nothing from this unbelievable feeling of suddenly moving about freely, without grinding my teeth in pain. If this is coming from you, you are a very powerful healer. No words of thankfulness can be enough to respond to this miracle."

He signed himself, "Thankful . . . and deeply puzzled."

Later, when I explained to him that I have no special powers, I gave the credit to "Mother Nature" flowing through me. His skeptical opinions had been shaken, but "Divine Mother" still seemed like too much of a stretch. Watching him now—months later, still moving around without pain—perhaps someday I will tell him.

—from Tyagini Naima

ANGEL WINGS

Coughing, sneezing, nose running, head aching—my physical condition was a perfect reflection of my mental state. If ever there was a day designed for staying in bed with a cup of tea and a good book, this was it! But it wasn't going to happen.

For months I had been working out the details of a group pilgrimage to India—the first one I'd arranged. This morning, final decisions had to be made and a price agreed upon. The arrangements, complicated enough in themselves, were made more confusing by the cross-cultural issues. I was working with good people in India; but concepts like "Now" or "Yes, definitely I will do it" meant something quite different there than they did in America.

I was sitting in front of my computer, doing the best I could with my anxious mind and uncooperative body, when the bell rang for noon meditation. (I work in the office of Ananda's Meditation Retreat.)

It was hard to imagine sitting for meditation in my present condition, but an inner voice said, "Go to the temple." So I staggered over there and plopped down on the floor without even a cushion, too tired to get one from the closet or move a chair from the stack against the wall.

I stayed in the back, thinking I might have to leave quickly if a fit of sneezing or coughing overcame me. Deep meditation seemed impossible, so I surrendered completely to feeling overwhelmed and terrible. "I'll just sit here and watch the breath," I thought. It was the best I could do.

All of a sudden I was lifted into a higher state. I don't usually see anything notable when I meditate; but now with inner vision I saw the huge, white wings of an angel, which, in my vision, wrapped around me, lifted me up, and comforted me.

My nose stopped running. The headache went away. No hint of sneezing or coughing. I was in a state of absolute peace.

The word that came to me was *Shechina*. It is a Hebrew word for Divine Mother that I learned growing up Jewish. Later I looked up the meaning: "Indwelling Place." That's where I was, dwelling in the sacred arms of Mother Divine.

I don't know how long I rested there. The meditation goes for thirty minutes, and when the end bell rang I heard it, and was conscious that people were leaving, but I stayed in the temple in the arms of Divine Mother for another twenty minutes or so. Gradually the experience went away; and there I was, sitting on the floor, nose running, head pounding again. But everything inside had changed. I couldn't even remember what I had been so concerned about! Feeling the grace of *Shechina*, I knew all would be well.

—from Diksha

I SING YOUR SONG

The big concert was on Saturday, and on Wednesday I lost my voice. I am part of a quartet that sings the music of Swami Kriyananda, and we had been months in planning and rehearsing for an interfaith "Unity through Music" event: an elegant dinner followed by a performance of our singing quartet. But it's a little hard to do four-part harmony with only three voices.

I tried every possible treatment—gargling, inhaling, and consuming a wide variety of concoctions—hoping something would work.

By Friday I could manage a few of the lower notes, but I had the tonal quality of a duck. I couldn't even rehearse with the group, yet the concert was twenty-four hours away. I knew Ananda friends around the world were praying for me. I wrote also to Swamiji and asked him to pray.

That night, before I went to bed, I opened at random Swamiji's autobiography, *The New Path*. There, in the last chapter, I found the following story:

"Many years ago," Swamiji wrote, "I felt that Divine Mother wanted me to return to India. I had been absent from there for ten years, but now

I had enough money saved to go back and stay there for about two months.

"Shortly before my scheduled departure, I was driving my car into San Francisco when the engine threw a rod. I realized I'd have to trade in this car for a newer one. This need, however, placed me in a dilemma. The money for my trip was all the wealth I had. Should I trade in my car and buy a new one? Or should I keep my money for the trip Divine Mother wanted me to take? I've always tried to reconcile faith with common sense.

"Ananda Village [where Swamiji lived] is in the mountains, far from urban conveniences. A car is, for me, a virtual necessity. I wouldn't be able to stay long in India. Without a vehicle, I'd be virtually 'stranded' upon my return. What should I do?

"I asked Divine Mother for guidance. I knew of no place in which to sit quietly and 'tune in.' All I could think of was to have a quiet lunch with a few friends in a downtown restaurant. No guidance came.

"Finally I said, 'Divine Mother, You haven't answered me; perhaps I haven't been silent enough to hear You. Common sense tells me, however, that I must have a car when I return from India. I see no reasonable choice, therefore, but to buy one. If You still want me to take this journey, You'll have to reimburse me!'

"I paid $1,100 for a good second-hand car. This money, along with $700 I received for my crippled vehicle, covered the cost. I left the car dealership on Friday evening. The next Monday morning, at home, I received a letter from someone unknown to me. Enclosed was a check—made out to me, personally—for a thousand dollars. The letter stated, 'Please use this money as Divine Mother wants you to.'

"Now, please ask yourself: How many people in America pray to God as their Divine Mother? Hardly any! Every time I recall this episode, my eyes fill with tears. Many, many times in my life have I found Divine Mother's loving assistance fulfilling my needs, answering my questions! In living for God, I have found the thrill of an unceasing, divine romance."

Everything about Swamiji's story thrilled me. He had been dealing with a new car and a trip to India, while my problem was laryngitis; but we intersected on one critical point: praying to Divine Mother. Swamiji had said to God, "If You still want me to take this journey, You'll have to reimburse me!"

What sweetness! What non-attachment!

Like Swamiji, I prayed, "Divine Mother, if you want me to sing, You will have to heal me." I continued with my gargling and inhaling, and everything else I could do, but now I put the results in Her hands.

Saturday morning showed slight improvement, but not nearly enough. Swamiji sent an email: "I am praying for you." Many times in the lives of others I had seen the power of Swamiji's prayers, but this was the first time I knew he was praying for me.

A few hours before the concert we had a sound check and a brief rehearsal, to see if the quartet would have to become a trio. I still sounded like a dying duck. Before giving up completely, we thought to try one verse of the song "Brothers."

The tenor starts, then the bass (me) joins in. This gave me another few seconds to pray again, "If You want me to sing, You are going to have to heal me." When it was time for me to join in, no more duck-like tones! My voice was almost normal.

The concert went beautifully in four-part harmony. Sometimes, though, it was hard for me to sing—not as a result of the laryngitis, but because of the waves of blessing I felt pouring over me. I'd known this music could heal my consciousness. Now I knew it could heal my body as well.

—from Peter Kretzmann

GONE

The pain in my chest was so intense I couldn't breathe. It felt like a heart attack, but it was on the wrong side.

I went into the bathroom, thinking that if I splashed water on my face it might help. I saw there a picture of Babaji. It says in *Autobiography of a Yogi*, "Anyone who says with reverence the name of Babaji draws to himself an instant blessing."

I wasn't thinking of those words. I wasn't even praying. I was just in so much pain I wanted to be close to him, so I held Babaji's picture against the pain in my chest.

Instantly, the pain stopped.

—from Carolina Viscogliosi

Never Too Late

My mother became a widow just after she turned twenty-five. She was left alone with three small children, my youngest brother still in diapers. Almost a year later she met Wally, who was also twenty-five. Always the romantic, he chose New Year's Eve to propose, and just after Valentine's Day for the wedding.

Wally never knew his biological father. His mother, just a teenager at the time, was coerced into a marriage which she left soon after Wally was born. His mother remarried, but her husband and son never got along. At seventeen, Wally struck out on his own.

He was determined to give us what he never had: a loving father. Even after my sister was born a few years later, Wally never made any distinction among the four of us. He was our *dad*; there was no *step*father in our home. Even my mother said, "He didn't marry *me*; he married *us*."

At the time he was managing a Chevron Gas station in San Francisco. It was typical of his generous, big-hearted nature that he would take on so much responsibility with such modest means. His talents were soon recognized and he received many promotions, eventually finding his ideal job as vice-president in charge of the company's philanthropy in Los Angeles.

My mother was religious by nature; and from a young age I, too, was devoted to God. Dad never talked to either of us about spirituality, but neither did he criticize or interfere. He was a happy agnostic who never felt the need, until his last year, to explore the spiritual side of life.

In late October 2001, at the relatively young age of sixty-five, Dad was told he had pancreatic cancer and only a few months to live. At the Thanksgiving table that year he thanked each one of us for sharing not only his life, but now also his death.

At one point during that holiday I saw my mother and father walking together hand in hand, admiring a tall pine tree covered with Christmas lights.

"Dear Divine Mother," I prayed. "She needs more time. We all need more time. Let my father live at least one more year so we can say a proper good-bye. And, if possible, awaken him to Your presence."

His changed circumstances made him spiritually receptive. I gave him several books that were important to me, including one, with a video, about how to meditate. He read them all, and watched the video many times.

Every night now, before he went to sleep, he practiced meditation. As the months passed he grew softer and sweeter, with a light in his eyes I had never seen before. We began to pray with him, and he didn't object. He let his Mormon and Catholic friends bless him and, when the time came, accepted last rites.

Just over a year after I had asked Divine Mother to extend his life, it was obvious the end was near. When the hospice worker came, Dad talked to him for an hour about his wonderful, and as he now called it, *blessed* life.

When my brother wept at the sight of my father's now emaciated frame, Dad comforted him. "It doesn't matter. The only thing that matters is the love we share."

In the last week, when he could no longer get out of bed, my brother-in-law asked him, "What do you think about as you lie there?"

"Succeeding," Dad said.

He was referring to his death. That he would die soon was self-evident. It was a question only of how calm, courageous, and uplifted he would be when the time came. My father knew that the same techniques he used to transcend the body when he meditated would also help him transition out of the body altogether.

From then on I noticed that Dad's eyes were often uplifted and focused on the spiritual eye at the point between the eyebrows, the way we do when we meditate.

In the last hours his eyes were open, unblinking, raised, and slightly rolled back, riveted now on the spiritual eye. When it came time for his last breath, I was sitting next to him with my hand on his forehead, praying, "Divine Mother, take him into the Light."

He departed calmly, his eyes fixed at the spiritual eye.

As a last good-bye, two tears fell from his eyes, which my mother caught in a handkerchief. "Oh, my darling husband," she said.

—from Kristy Fassler-Hecht

HARD LESSON

I don't know which was more important to me, the music or the drugs. I started playing drums when I was seven. Twenty years later I played jazz with Herbie Hancock, Latin with Cal Tjader, and I was on the same bill with Ten Years After. I was totally immersed in the San Francisco music scene. But if there had been no music, I think I still would have done the drugs.

I read *Autobiography of a Yogi* in 1969. I wanted a spiritual path, but without the hard work; especially when, instead, I could just get high. I used hard narcotics for about twelve years. Then one morning I woke up thinking, "I can't do this anymore." I was scrambling for money all the time, and the drugs themselves took such a toll on my body, mind, and spirit. I couldn't keep going that way.

For the next twelve years I went to AA. I never used drugs again.

In 1992 I went for a routine physical exam. The doctor found something in my blood he didn't like. Somewhere in those drug years I had picked up the virus Hepatitis C. I wasn't sick yet, but the doctor said eventually I would be. There was no cure.

Fast-forward another fifteen years. My life was going just fine. I rarely thought of the ticking time bomb inside of me. I had been carrying the virus around for thirty years and I was still exercising, enjoying my family, and carrying on as usual.

Most of the time Hepatitis C attacks your liver; but for some reason that the doctors couldn't explain, for me it was my kidneys. I did two cycles of interferon, a treatment similar to chemotherapy. The side effects were worse than the disease. My kidney function became so bad that they put me on the list for a transplant and started dialysis. The treatments were twice a week for two hours, but they seemed to last much longer. The average wait for a kidney was eight years. I couldn't imagine going on in this way.

I started spiraling down; my mood got darker and darker. Hepatitis C had taken away everything—exercise, food, sleep, work—everything. Finally I hit spiritual bottom and called to God in a way I never had before.

At that point the seed planted so many years before by *Autobiography of a Yogi* began to take root. My wife and I found an Ananda temple right near our home. We started attending regularly, taking classes, and meditating daily. Eventually, we received Kriya initiation.

I live by the ocean, and I started walking on the beach whenever I could. My wife suggested four words to me: "Manifest Thy Healing Presence." I started saying the words over and over. I was saying them so much that when I *didn't*, it was a big event.

Doctors were monitoring my condition. Suddenly, everything seemed to be getting better.

"Let's try it without dialysis," the doctor said. He didn't have to twist my arm. I had stopped before, but it had never lasted more than a few weeks.

It has been six months now without dialysis, and my kidney function has been getting better one day at a time. Six months is not a year, a decade, or a lifetime, but it is a *lot* longer that I have ever gone before.

The doctors have no explanation, but I can explain it in four words: "Manifest Thy Healing Presence."

—from David Leland

HANDS ACROSS
the SEA

W hat had been chronic back pain for this middle-aged business-
man suddenly became much worse. Even with morphine, the
pain was so excruciating he couldn't stand straight. Scans revealed bone
overgrowth and fused vertebrae. Too much "fine living," evidenced by
his ample body, had caught up with him. He was admitted into the hospital, then booked on an air ambulance to fly the next morning from our
small island to the mainland for emergency surgery.

A work colleague had recommended that he see me. I am known in
our community as a healer, but I say it is God who heals. When the man
took this sudden turn for the worse he had to cancel our appointment.

I woke the next morning with him on my mind. In meditation, I
felt time and distance disappear in the realm of spirit. I imagined him in
front of me as I prayed for his higher good. As is usual when I serve in
this way, immense energy flowed through me as my hands were gently
guided to direct energy where God knew it was needed.

When the healing was done, for some reason I felt I should tell the
man about it. He was on the mainland and I was on the island, so I

wrote him a letter. A few days later he called. I assumed he wanted to thank me for my prayers in his hour of need.

"You don't understand," he said. "Until I received your letter, nothing made any sense!"

He was taken to the aircraft in a wheelchair, he explained, heavily dosed on morphine but still in terrible pain. Halfway through the twenty-minute flight, he told his wife, "Something strange is happening." When they landed a few minutes later, he stood straight up and walked off the plane, stooping only to climb down the steps, his back perfectly pliable. The pain had vanished.

An ambulance was waiting on the tarmac to take him to the hospital. He accepted the ride, but felt like a fraud for doing so. It was even more awkward and embarrassed when he had to tell the orthopedic surgeon that his back felt just fine.

New scans revealed only perfectly normal vertebrae. Neither he nor the doctor had any explanation.

—from Maitreyi

One Life
Beneath *the* Surface

When we pulled into our driveway a police car pulled in right behind us. He must have been waiting for us. After quickly verifying our identities, he gave us the news.

"Your son has been in a serious accident. He has a head injury and is in critical condition. Here are the numbers to call."

Ben had been riding his bicycle down a steep hill, when a car suddenly turned left in front of him. He smashed into it going about thirty miles an hour. He was airborne for some twenty-five feet before the back of his head slammed into the pavement.

He was not wearing a helmet.

Now he was going in and out of consciousness in the ICU at the Albany New York Medical Center, four hours from our home in southern Maine. He had a fractured skull, multiple bleeds in his brain, and twelve staples on the back of his head, closing a large laceration.

As we gathered what we needed for the trip to Albany, we contacted friends and relatives, activating every prayer network we knew.

Inwardly I talked continuously to Divine Mother. "Ben is Your child.

I'm his mother in this life, but eternally he belongs to You. I surrender to Your will for him, whatever it may be." Then I added, "You are going to have to handle this through me. I cannot do this alone."

When we got to the Medical Center it was past midnight. About thirty of Ben's friends were in the waiting room, anxious to know how he was doing. Medical information could not be released to anyone but his family.

In the ICU, Ben was wired into all the most advanced medical devices. He was pale, but otherwise seemed to be sleeping peacefully. Whether asleep or unconscious, I could feel Ben was present. His soul had not separated from his body.

Softly I stroked his hair, saying over and over again, "You'll be fine. You'll be fine." This was partly affirmation, and partly a true expression of a growing hope I felt inside.

After several hours I simply had to go to the hotel room reserved for us, to get some rest. My husband stayed with Ben, so I felt free to leave. And I felt Divine Mother also there, watching over him.

I slept briefly and fitfully, then got up to pray and meditate. To my immense relief, I felt Divine Mother reassuring me, "Ben will recover."

From then on nothing could shake my faith. Alone in the hotel room I sang Swamiji's song, "Brothers"—especially moved by the lines: *One Life beneath the surface binds every man to me. Who knows himself knows all men as brothers.*

When I thought of Ben's friends sitting vigil in the waiting room, and of Swamiji and our Ananda friends worldwide praying for him, tears of gratitude spilled down my cheeks.

Interestingly, at the same time Divine Mother was reassuring me, the doctor was preparing my husband for the worst. "Your son is in *critical* condition!" he emphatically declared.

The next morning, even though his eyes were closed and he was in a semi-conscious state, Ben must have sensed my presence or recognized my voice.

"Hi, Mama," he whispered.

We had sent Swamiji a photo of Ben, taken in the ICU. Swamiji's secretary told us Swamiji looked at it intently for several minutes, then said quietly, "He'll be okay."

For ten days Ben stayed in the Medical Center, moving in and out of consciousness. Sometimes, in his periods of wakefulness, Ben felt waves of love, both human and divine, washing over him. Often he wept with gratitude.

The dear man whose car Ben had smashed into had been so traumatized by the accident that he couldn't bear to come to the hospital until it was clear that Ben would survive.

"I don't know if you believe in God," he said with tears in his eyes, "but I know God is real, and He is watching out for all of us."

Three and a half weeks later, Ben came home.

"When I think of how fast I was going on that bike, how far I flew, and how hard my head hit the pavement, I have no explanation for why I am alive, or why I have recovered so quickly," he said. "Many others at the hospital, whose accidents were far less severe than mine, are suffering much more than I. It doesn't add up. But here I am. So somehow it must."

For a long time Ben's peers had been more important to him than his parents. Now he seemed content just to be home with us, sharing the kind of time parents rarely have with an almost-grown son. At times we feared it was "lack of initiative," one of the lingering effects of traumatic brain injury. Mostly, though, we felt (and Ben concurred) that the accident had given him an expanded perspective on everything. There was a special tenderness to our relationship during these months of recovery.

I have had a serious spiritual practice since before Ben was born, so he has often been exposed to meditation and the Ananda teachings I follow. But now he started looking into them on his own. He had been on the receiving end of the power of prayer and wanted to find out more about that dimension of life.

In May 2012, for the first time since he was a child, Ben came with me to Ananda Village in California for a long weekend celebrating Swami Kriyananda's eighty-sixth birthday.

At a special dinner, Ben and I sat across the room from Swamiji. Even though his body is frail, and he rarely walks unassisted, when Swamiji heard we were there, he rose from his chair and with great effort came to greet Ben.

Ben rose to welcome Swamiji and for some time they stood, wrapped in each other's arms, while the whole room watched in reverent silence.

"When I was in the hospital," Ben told Swamiji, "I felt such love and deep interconnectedness with all of life. Many times I wept."

"I feel that too," Swamiji replied.

After dinner, Ben said to me, "Whatever you did, however you got me to come here, thank you."

All I had done was invite him as I had many times before, since he became old enough to make his own decisions. He was the one who was different. This time he said "Yes."

—*from Kristy Fassler–Hecht*

Not *for* Myself, Lord

I t was a Sunday morning, and I had the worship service to conduct in our temple at eleven o'clock.

At nine o'clock, I had a sudden kidney stone attack. It was the most intense pain I have ever experienced. My body was shaking like a leaf. Friends tried to persuade me to let them drive me to the nearest hospital, but that would have meant going some twenty-five miles on a winding road. The very thought was—well, unthinkable!

A principle of mine is, in suffering, not to pray for myself. I'll pray for others, but to pray for personal relief seems to me an admission that I am attached to this ego, and this I won't do. I have dedicated my life to the practice of seeing God, in everything, as the Doer. Accordingly, I sat there, trembling, too much in pain even to speak.

At a certain point, I looked at my watch. 10:45. I'd been enduring this unbelievably intense pain for an hour and three quarters. Now I thought of a way of praying that would not be for myself, but for others.

"Divine Mother," my prayer went, "the worship service is about to begin. If you want me to conduct it, You will have to take this pain away!"

In the length of time it takes to inhale one breath, the pain simply disappeared! It was replaced by a joy so intense that, still, I could hardly speak! But I was able to conduct the service, and though I wept throughout my sermon, my tears expressed the intense joy I felt, not my former pain.

—from Swami Kriyananda

Dear Cancer Cells...

"I have to get out of here!" I said to my husband, as I grabbed keys, jacket, and cell phone.

"Do you want me to go with you?" he asked.

"No!" I was right on the edge of full-blown panic as I ran out the door.

When I have an anxiety attack, I feel like running as far and as fast as I can. This time I went about a mile to the edge of the lake near our home before I could stop and consider what was going on in my mind.

There was a reason for me to be afraid. It was two days before Christmas and I had just been diagnosed with stage four metastasized cancer. The doctor was going to call this afternoon with the results of the PET scan, which would tell us where the cancer had started and how far it had spread.

"This could be my last Christmas!" I thought. "I might never sit by this lake again, or kayak in the water, or watch my grandkids play here." Panic was overcoming me. I wanted to scream.

"Stop it!" I told myself. "If this were happening to your sister or one of your friends, what would you say to help them get through?" In the past I had often been able to help others through difficult times. Now all I had to offer myself was fear. I took a couple of deep breaths.

"Give the cancer to God," I responded, carrying both sides of the dialogue.

"But to give it to God," I protested, "I would first have to *own* the cancer and I don't want to have anything to do with it!" Once again panic was rising.

Suddenly, standing in front of me a little to the left, as clear and solid as the trees behind him, I saw my Guru, Paramhansa Yogananda.

"*Offer up your fear*," he said.

Cupping my hands in front of my heart, I visualized the fear that filled me from my toes to the top of my head. I saw it flowing out of my body and into my hands, which I held up to him.

"Thank you for taking this," I said.

A wave of peace and love came over me. I walked home, cheerfully greeting my neighbors, "Merry Christmas. Merry Christmas." In stark contrast to the panic- driven flight before.

"Hi Honey, I'm home," I called to my husband, as I went in the door. "I'm going to put on a pot of coffee. Do you want some?"

The cancer turned out to be serious indeed. I spent many days in the hospital and several times nearly died. Through it all, however, I was almost never afraid. I felt Divine Mother's presence within me, and flowing through all my caregivers.

Once, during what I thought would be a routine examination, the doctor suddenly grabbed the phone, called the Diagnostic Imaging Center and said, "I'm sending a patient down to you. Get her in *immediately*!" I had a blood clot he thought was heading for my heart.

Fear started to rise within me. Fortunately my husband thought to call the "prayer hotline" at Ananda and ask for immediate help. By the time I got to the Imaging Center, I felt a wave of peace sweeping over me from the prayers being offered on my behalf. I was no longer afraid. If I had died then, or been told death was imminent, I knew it would be fine.

"I have done what I need to do here," I thought. "God will take care of the rest." I don't know how people make it through an experience like this without faith in God.

I've always been a purist when it comes to food and medicine, shunning allopathic in favor of more natural healing methods. Now I had to surrender all of that. Every time I took chemotherapy, I said grace over the chemo bag as if it were a meal I was about to enjoy. I wrote a special prayer:

"Divine Mother, receive this chemo in Thy Light. Infuse it with Your Love, Your Light, and Your Divine Healing power. With deep gratitude I accept this gift and expect only the highest good to come of it. With deep gratitude I anticipate the possible side-effects to be minimal or nonexistent. Thank You, God. Thy will be done."

I would visualize the medication flowing through my body as healing energy, gathering up the darkness (cancer cells) and leading them to the Light for transmutation. I also addressed the cancer cells directly.

"Dear cancer cells within my body: I thank you for the messages you have given me. Your presence is no longer required in my body and I ask you to leave now. I gently release you into the Light."

Despite my prayers, I did lose my hair. On the morning I knew it was going to happen, I was afraid even to comb it. I shed a few tears, and tried all the usual clichés—"It's just *hair*. It will grow back. No more bad hair days."—but nothing worked. I needed something positive to hold onto. I decided that every clump of hair represented an equal amount of cancer cells leaving my body. It took about an hour to comb all the hair out. It was not a time of sorrow. It was releasing, renewing, and joy.

I've been cancer-free for over a year now. My life has changed completely. I had spent most of my life worrying about everything, especially my daughter who has an incurable disease. Repeatedly over the last twenty-five years she has been in and out of the hospital.

Every time the phone rang or there was a knock at the door, I expected it to be bad news about her. I wouldn't go anywhere without a cell phone. If the phone didn't work, I would be almost in a panic that something would happen to her and I wouldn't know.

I love my daughter and all my family the same as before, but now I know that they belong to Divine Mother as much as they belong to me. She will care for them, whether or not I am here to help Her. I am at peace with that.

For six months during the cancer treatment I couldn't swallow anything—neither food nor water. A feeding tube kept me alive. Now even a sip of water is cause for rejoicing.

After it was over—when the cancer was gone, the treatments were done, and my hair had grown back—I spent a long time finding just the right words to tell others what it all meant to me.

One day...
she decided to let go of her fear and her past
and live only in the present
  moment.
She opened her eyes
and saw beauty everywhere.
She opened her heart
and found herself surrounded
by love and compassion.
She searched within and realized
that happiness comes and goes
but joy and inner peace are inherent.
That day
she chose freedom
and found that she could fly.

—from Cheryl Mack

GOD COMES

*"In whatever way I am approached,
in that way do I respond.
All men come, by whatever path, to Me."*

BHAGAVAD GITA
~ Chapter 4, Verse 11 ~

GRANDPA
and the LADY

I was still in my mother's womb when my grandfather passed away. Even though I never met him, he exerted a strong spiritual influence over my life. My mother's love for him was the living link between us. That and the family stories I heard from a young age. My favorite was the one about the Lady.

My grandfather grew up in a poor area of Italy not far from Naples. When he reached early manhood there was no job and no money, so he left for America. It was 1901; he was nineteen years old. He settled in an Italian neighborhood in New York City where he lived for the rest of his life.

He had neither an education nor a trade, so most of his working life was manual labor. When he grew too old for physical work he became the caretaker at a cemetery.

One evening, after the cemetery was closed and the gate was locked, he saw a lovely young woman walking among the gravestones. She was about sixteen years old, dressed in white. When he tried to speak to her, she smiled, then playfully ran away. He followed her, but she played hide and seek with him. He never found out who she was or why she was there.

He thought about her often in the several months before she returned. Again, it was after hours, the gate was locked. This time she was dressed in blue.

"Who are you?" he asked. "How did you get in?"

"Who do you think I am?" she said, answering him in his own Neapolitan dialect.

He was so startled he couldn't move, overwhelmed by her beauty and the love emanating from her. By the time he recovered, she was gone.

After that, he thought of her constantly and looked for her every day. Several months passed before she returned. This time she was dressed in black.

"You are the Blessed Mother," he said to her. "No other lady could be so beautiful and fill me with such joy. Please don't go away."

"Soon I will take you home with me," she said.

When he got back to his house that night he gathered his family around him, including my mother, with me in her womb. He told them about the Lady.

"Soon I am going to die," he said. They knew he was telling the truth, but they could hardly believe it. Four days later the Lady kept her promise. In the middle of the night, my grandfather had a heart attack and died.

—from Mary Mintey

PICTURE PERFECT

By the time the young man arrived, the room was so full that the only place left for him to sit was on the floor against the back wall. This was no problem for him, and he settled down comfortably to listen to Swami Kriyananda speak.

The venue was a metaphysical bookstore in Southern California. The lecture hall was lined with pictures of great spiritual teachers, ancient and modern, East and West, whose teachings also filled the bookshelves.

The young man was hoping to get clarity this evening on a question that had been preoccupying him of late. He was deeply drawn to the guru, Sathya Sai Baba. He had read many of his books and spent time with his American devotees, entranced by their stories of being with "Baba" in India. The man wanted to go to India to see Baba, but he was afraid.

"What if I am disappointed? After all that effort and expense, I would be so sad and embarrassed in front of my friends. Is Baba my guru? How can I be sure?"

About midway through his lecture, Swamiji began to speak about the need for a guru. "You can't do it on your own. You need the help of a guru."

Someone in the audience asked a question. "How am I going to find my guru?"

"You don't have to travel the world looking for him," Swamiji said. "If your search is sincere, your guru will come to you right here."

When Swamiji said the words "right here," one of the portraits fell off the wall and landed face up on the young man's lap. It was Sathya Sai Baba. He grabbed the picture and, with tears in his eyes, held it to his heart.

—from Asha

AM I NOT
ALWAYS *with* YOU?

For my job I had to spend a lot of time driving, but I didn't mind. I had been given a huge stash of Ananda classes on tape, and in the car I listened to those tapes over and over. As long as the Ananda teachers were speaking, everything felt right. But when I had to turn off the tape and get out of the car, life hit me full-blown, and it was a little more than I could handle easily.

I ran my own business, doing landscape maintenance for about sixty clients. It was enough to support my wife and three young children, but I had to work six days a week to make ends meet. Most of the responsibility for our local Ananda center also fell on my shoulders.

Work, family, meditation, taking care of the center—huff, puff! Even with cutting back on sleep, there was never enough time. I took to heart the words of Sri Yukteswar from *Autobiography of a Yogi*: "Everything in future will improve if you are making the right spiritual effort now." But I wanted that future to be now!

One day, walking fast, late for an appointment, I noticed a crumpled piece of newspaper lying on the ground about fifteen feet to the side from where I was walking. Acting on an impulse, I went over to pick it up.

"What are you doing?" I chided myself. "It isn't your duty to keep America litter-free!"

I lifted the paper from the sidewalk, smoothed it open, and saw it was a picture of my Guru, Paramhansa Yogananda.

—from Ramu

A Dark and Stormy Night

The decision to walk home late that night did not, at first, seem like a foolish one. It was only a mile to the lodge where I was staying, down a quiet rural road on a ridgetop outside of Assisi, Italy. There was no traffic at that hour, and there were no bad characters to fear. I had come to Assisi to "walk in the footsteps of St. Francis," and while I didn't know for sure that he had followed the path I was on, it was certain he had gone on foot around Assisi, as I was now doing.

For a while the reflected glow from the temple I had just left was enough to light my way. But the farther I walked, the darker it became. There were only a few houses in the area, and everyone seemed to have gone to bed. The sky was heavily overcast with no hint of moon or stars. Soon, I could just barely make out the line where the pavement met the gravel shoulder.

I began to feel nervous. To still my beating heart, I sang quietly to myself, "Sri Yogananda, guide to inner freedom, steal into my heart of hearts. Banish my delusions."

Surrounded by that song I felt less anxious, until it occurred to me that in this blackness I wouldn't be able to see the narrow driveway that led to the lodge. I could walk right past it and never know.

Just then, off to the right, I saw a firefly. I stopped to watch. I had never seen fireflies before arriving in Assisi a few days earlier. St. Francis had had a special reverence for God in Nature, so it seemed appropriate that I should meet these magical creatures for the first time here.

The firefly passed in front of me, and then hovered on my left. In the faint glow of his luminous body, I saw the entrance to the driveway. He stayed with me all the way to the door of the lodge, then flitted away.

Just as I stepped inside and closed the double doors behind me, a torrential rain began to fall.

—from Manisha

HANSA

I fell sixteen feet from a pull-down staircase and landed headfirst on a concrete floor. Fortunately, the only lasting injury was that I lost my senses of taste and smell.

"The goal of meditation is to overcome the senses," a meditating yogi-friend said to me. "Look at the bright side: Now you have two of them licked."

She knew that I had a good sense of humor and would take her comment in the right way. For me, however, this was more than an inconvenience. I was a professional chef, running my own café. All of that seemed over now. The doctors' prognosis was, if these senses didn't come back in eighteen months, the condition would be permanent.

Eight years passed and nothing changed. I was a disciple of Paramhansa Yogananda, practicing Kriya meditation. It was a comfort to know that whatever happened to me, God was in charge.

I moved from Vancouver Island to Ananda Village in California. When my husband wanted to move back to the island to start an Ananda center there, I was conflicted, but in the end, went with him.

Nine months later, ten days before my fiftieth birthday, my husband left me. Turns out we had moved to the island because it was the right setting for the marriage to fall apart.

It was my habit every morning to walk the block from our house, go down the stairs to the waterfront, and take a long stroll on the boardwalk. On the day he left, sad as I was, I followed the same routine.

I had a passing acquaintance with an elderly man named John who went out every morning the same as I. This day he was coming up the stairs as I was going down.

John was a "birder," and announced enthusiastically, "There is a trumpeter swan out there, all by himself."

"Alone?" I said. These birds were seldom seen on this part of the island, and never alone. Always they were with their mates.

"All by himself," John repeated.

When I got to the boardwalk, there he was, a magnificent creature one hundred feet from the shore.

In India the swan is a symbol of spiritual realization, perhaps because it is at home on land, air, and sea, just as a spiritual master is at home in the three worlds: causal, astral, and material. My Guru's title, "Paramhansa," literally means "supreme swan." It is conferred only on those who have the highest state of Self-realization.

To see a swan on this particular day, alone without a mate—as I was now—I took as a sign that Master had not forgotten me. Even though my heart was wounded, I felt an expansive joy. Breathing deeply, I savored the moment.

To my astonishment, I could smell the sea! I thought it was an astral phenomenon. Perhaps the swan, too, was not really there, but only a vision from the astral world. Then I remembered that John had also seen him. Again I breathed deeply of the ocean air. This time it carried the mixed-fragrance of fish, kelp, and the usual rotting debris.

Amazed, I began to weep, not because my sense of smell had returned, but in gratitude for Master's presence in my life.

When I got home, I followed my morning ritual. Fixing a cup of coffee, I took it out onto the porch. To my amazement, I could both smell and taste the brew. My senses had returned.

I last saw the swan far out in the water, moving away from shore. At the time, I thought nothing of it. Later I understood that he was beckoning me, leading me away from the island back to my home at Ananda Village.

—*from Jyoti*

Now!

Those who regularly smoke marijuana like to say that "pot" isn't habit forming. Maybe you don't get the "shaking frenzy" like you do when you stop drinking alcohol, or the horrors that come with heroin withdrawal. That doesn't mean that marijuana is easy to quit. Especially if you have been using it a lot, for years, as I had been doing.

Many times I quit "forever" only to start up again in a few days or weeks. I wanted so much more for myself than the life I had. The first step, I knew, was to give up smoking pot.

I came down with a bad chest cold. At least it kept me from smoking. I had a bag of marijuana, but because of the cold I hadn't touched it. Then I started getting better and the desire to smoke returned. I was reaching for the pipe when I remembered my repeated resolutions to give this up and make a better life for myself.

I had my hand on the bag when, through the ether, a deep, resonant voice boomed out, "YOU MUST QUIT NOW!" My hand started shaking and I dropped the bag onto the floor.

There was a copy of *Autobiography of a Yogi* on my bookshelf, but I hadn't read it. The cover photo of Paramhansa Yogananda had attracted me, and I often gazed at his picture. Years later, when I heard for the first time a recording of Yogananda's voice, I recognized it immediately as the voice that had given me the order—and, as it turned out, also the courage—to "QUIT NOW."

In all my previous efforts to quit, I had always first finished the bag in hand. This time I returned the bag to the man who had sold it to me, along with the pipe and all the other paraphernalia. I have never smoked pot again.

—from Anonymous

MORE THAN
a LIFETIME

When age-related dementia sets in, people often go either sweet or angry, depending on how they have lived. My dad was a very competitive guy—a trial attorney, inclined to live on the angry side. When he was diagnosed with Alzheimer's, I assumed my siblings and I were in for a hard time. To our delight he went sweet, I think because Mom was helping him from the other side.

Mom had died seven years earlier, after fifty-six years of marriage to Dad. He was devoted to her. When she had a sudden cardiac and respiratory failure, she was on life support for three days. Previously she had made her wishes clear: "When the quality of life is gone, when the doctors say there is no hope of recovery, please let me go." Clearly that moment had come. Dad knew this was the right decision, but when we took her off life support he was devastated.

Mom must have known he wasn't ready to let her go, so instead of dying as we all expected, she began to breathe on her own. She was conscious and aware of what was going on around her, but her brain had been oxygen deprived and she suffered from aphasia. Verbal communication was scrambled. Most of the time she couldn't use words in a sensible way.

We took her home where she lived another seven months. My father surprised us all, becoming her tender, fulltime caregiver. Somehow they managed to communicate, and my father told me that often when she first woke up in the morning her expression was like that of a newborn baby.

"She was talking to angels," my father said. "Of course I couldn't see them, so I would ask her, 'How many are there?' She would point to each one as she counted."

My mother was a devout Catholic. My father rarely went to church. His father had been a Congregational minister. "My dad was my main connection to God," my father told me, on one of the rare occasions when we talked about it. "Now that he's gone, I prefer to commune with God in Nature."

I think my mother also connected my dad to God. Dad and I were with her when she peacefully breathed her last. A few minutes later, through our tears, we saw that her expression had changed to a beatific smile. Dad was ecstatic.

"I had asked her to give me a sign from the other side," he told me, "to let me know she was okay." Her smile, he felt, was that sign.

After her death he would still talk to her in the evenings, he said, and she would answer him. Later, when he had a terminal diagnosis himself and hospice was called in, and his Alzheimer's got worse, he was surprisingly calm and peaceful.

My sister, however, was worried that Dad might not be at peace with God. She wanted us to talk to him about his relationship with Jesus and with God.

My father rarely talked about God, and I didn't think he would welcome such a conversation now. My beliefs are different from my sister's, but on this we agreed: We both wanted Dad to die peacefully, unafraid, with a conscious connection to the divine. I prayed for a way to talk to him about death and what happens afterwards. My mother provided the bridge.

"Have you been talking to Mom recently?" I asked him one evening. He seemed particularly peaceful, and I thought that must be the reason.

"Yes," he said quietly.

"What did she say?" I asked.

"That it is not quite time for me to go," he replied.

"Really?" I said, trying to hide my surprise. "Did she say anything else?"

"Yes. That when my time comes, she'll help me."

That settled the question for me and, fortunately, also for my sister.

"When it comes time for him to die," I suggested to her, "Tell him to go into the light, to God, and also to Mom. She'll take him where he needs to go."

Not long after, with my sister and I by his side, Dad peacefully passed away.

—from Mangala

SAVED

From the beginning of my discipleship to Master, I tried to develop with him a personal relationship, to remember him at all times. Sometimes I succeeded; more often I forgot.

One night I went to bed after meditating as usual, and a few hours later found myself in the worst nightmare I have ever had. Malevolent people, dark forces attacking me, frightening noise: it was a perfect picture of hell!

Just when I was about to be beheaded, somehow, even in my subconscious state, I had the presence of mind to call out, "Master!"

Maybe some part of me remembered the story Swamiji told of finding himself in the presence of a dark entity and feeling his consciousness being sucked into that darkness. "Master!" Swamiji had said, and instantly the darkness disappeared.

For me, too, the result was instantaneous. I woke up sweating and trembling, but safe in my own bed.

Unpleasant though it was, that experience was very encouraging to me. I was new and inexperienced, but still, in a moment of need, I remembered to call on Master. And he responded instantly, for he is always there.

—*from Sadhana Devi*

VALENTINE

I was at the beach. The tide was going out when I drew a big heart in the dry sand, well above the wave line. "I love you, Divine Mother!!!!" I wrote inside it. Turning to the ocean I said, "Now, KISS me!" Then I stood waiting for God to respond.

Soon a rogue wave came all the way up to where I was standing—and took my heart and my message off the beach and out into the infinite sea.

—*from Anonymous*

VEHICLE *for* *the* DIVINE

Even before we were introduced, I felt intensely drawn to the man who became my husband. He was a decade older, from another country and culture. I spoke none of his native language, and he knew only a little of mine. We met in a park in New York City, and the man who introduced us was himself a stranger to me.

I had just finished my freshman year at Columbia University and was not quite twenty years old.

The second time we met he handed me a copy of *Autobiography of a Yogi*. Not because of any interest on his part; he had found it lying in the street and passed it on to me.

I was the daughter of an atheist, but had recently come to believe in the existence of God. I was intrigued by the book and thought the author, pictured on the cover, looked interesting. But the man who had handed me the book interested me far more. So, after reading a few pages, I put *Autobiography of a Yogi* aside.

The man and I spent one exhilarating month together. In my infatuation I missed all the warning signs, and didn't realize that marriage to him would be a nightmare of physical and mental abuse, poverty, sickness, and isolation.

Finally, one night I prayed with all my heart and soul for God's help.

Almost immediately, circumstances changed. I was able to trade my housecleaning services for a yoga class. I met a teacher there who tutored me in meditation and *pranayama*. I began creeping out of bed at 4:30 in the morning to do my practices.

I felt, after that night of desperate prayer, that God had grabbed me by the scruff of the neck and was pulling me away from the self-destructive path I had been following for more than a decade.

One night after a meditation class, instead of just saying good-bye, the teacher insisted on escorting me to my car. I had rarely been alone with a man who was not my husband. There was a full moon, and for a moment we stood together in awkward silence. Then he said, "Sister, you are in an abusive marriage and it is time you woke up!"

At that exact instant, the headlights of my car began to flash and the horn honked repeatedly. I had an electronic key, but years earlier the battery had worn out and I had never replaced it.

Soon after, I confronted my husband. We were outside, standing next to my car, when I issued my declaration of independence from his abusive ways. Once again the headlights flashed and the horn honked.

I looked right at him and said, "I'm not the only one who knows what you've been doing."

His response a few days later was to attack me in a drunken rage. I thought it might be my last day on earth. The next night I left and never returned.

Several days later I met a friend who had with her a copy of *Autobiography of a Yogi*. This time I read it, cherishing every word, weeping with joy and thanksgiving, at times so moved I could scarcely breathe.

I realize now that Divine Mother was always with me during those dark and difficult years. She was playing in my heart, urging me to awaken. And when I finally called to Her, She responded—thankfully, loud and clear!

—from Premi

Right Number

was raised in India, in a very conservative family. I believed deeply in God and the protective power of a guru, and sensed this greater reality around me at all times. Yet I found it difficult to relate to life and became very introverted. With my family and friends, and even after I married and had children, my heart still longed for something deeper.

One day I heard about Ananda Sangha in India and felt a deep calling toward that path. I saw Swami Kriyananda on the Aasta television channel and wrote down the contact number when it flashed on the screen.

At 7:00 a.m. on January 2, 2004, I called the number. Swami Kriyananda answered the phone. For a teacher of his unique stature and worldwide fame, he is very accessible. Still, I was told later, he *never* answered that phone. It was the public number for all of Ananda in India, and others took care of those calls. He was rarely even *near* that phone, especially at that time of the morning.

He introduced himself only as the author of the books that Ananda publishes. I recognized his voice instantly, though, and told him, "I know who you are." I meant more than just his name. In him I knew I had found the teacher I had been searching for all my life. Without hesitation I poured out to him the deepest longings of my heart. We talked for only fifteen minutes, but it was long enough to confirm what I had known the moment he picked up the phone. I had found my Guru, my path, and my spiritual home.

—from Sangeeta

RESCUED

I remember the exact moment I decided to kill myself. It was late in the evening. I was lying on my bed. All the drugs and alcohol I'd been taking for years couldn't touch the black hopelessness that was my life. Death was the only way out.

I was twenty-three years old. I settled myself into the not-unwelcome thought that my life would soon be over.

Suddenly I felt a strong presence hovering over me. Clearly spoken into my physical ear, I heard the word, "NO!"

Instantly, I knew there was a plan for my life and it was not suicide.

A deep peace came over me. Deeper and more profound than anything I had known before.

From that point I was guided, step-by-step, to everything I needed to change my life.

—from Anonymous

RAINFALL *and*
MOONLIGHT

It was not the custom in South America, where I was raised, for students to work during the breaks between school terms. But when I went to college and the three-week vacation came, I felt it was time to get a job. I wanted to make an offering to Divine Mother, to spend the entire three weeks communing with God. I would find some kind of physical work that would leave my mind free to think only of Her.

I got a job in a manufacturing plant that made steel containers. For ten hours a day, four days a week, from 3:30 in the afternoon until 1:30 in the morning, I pulled finished containers out of the oven as the paint dried, stacked them in twos and fours, then loaded them onto a moveable cart. It was hot, hard work.

It was also blissful, at least at first. The plant was so noisy that I could chant "O God Beautiful" at full voice without disturbing anyone.

I commuted to work on my bicycle. In the afternoons I followed a beautiful trail through the woods. At night, however, even with a full moon, under the overhanging trees it was so dark that I couldn't see the path and had to take a much less-congenial route down a main street.

At the end of the first week, I felt my effort to be with Divine Mother had been a grand success. When the second week began, however, I noticed a marked decline in my feeling of bliss. Physically I was exhausted, being completely unaccustomed to this kind of labor. With fatigue came a loss of faith in my ability to keep my promise to God. Self-doubt proved to be self-fulfilling. I was never able to recapture the bliss I had at the beginning. I felt like a spiritual failure. In the middle of that second week, when I got home, I had a complete breakdown.

Somehow I pulled myself together enough to make it through the rest of the week and the one that followed. Those were long hard days. Fatigue and discouragement were my enemies, but I fought against them and kept Divine Mother with me as much as I could. I continued to chant mentally when I couldn't summon the strength to use my voice.

I was very sad and told Divine Mother how disappointed I was that I hadn't been able to keep Her constantly with me. Still, I had done my best, and on the last day I asked for some reassuring sign of Her favor.

"Perhaps," I said, "we can ride home together. Not on the busy street, but through the forest path." Maybe it was a foolish prayer. Even with a full moon I had found it was too dark to ride there.

When I came out of the factory at the end of my shift, I was astonished to see a thin layer of rain clouds covering the entire sky, forming perfect "light panels" reflecting the moonlight everywhere. It looked like twilight rather than the middle of the night.

As I rode down the forest path, easily visible, a soft rain began to fall, lifting from me the exhaustion of the last three weeks. I felt Divine Mother's presence telling me, "By doing your best to keep Me always in your heart, by never giving up despite the setbacks, you have pleased Me very much."

—*from Hezequiel*

My Child

When my husband left me for the minister of my church, naturally I found another church to attend. Out of loyalty to me, and upset over what had happened, many of my friends left too, and soon we were happily settled in a new spiritual home. So when my daughter moved to Ananda Village, I just came to see what she was up to, not out of any spiritual need of my own.

This daughter and I have always been close—spiritually, and in every other way—so when she suggested I read *Autobiography of a Yogi*, I didn't hesitate. In my church they told us to meditate, but never taught us how to do it. In *Autobiography of a Yogi* I saw the promise of meditation in a way I had never heard of before.

Ananda also had a center in the city where I lived, but I traveled a lot for work and could never attend their meditation classes. The leader gave me a special Saturday session, and from that point my spiritual life began to change.

Still, I was concerned. "Is this really my path, or am I doing this just to be close to my daughter?" I went on for a long time in this way, a house divided. I just couldn't make up my mind.

Finally, on New Year's Eve 1985, I went to the local Ananda service. I prayed to Paramhansa Yogananda, "Master, you just have to tell me. Am I doing this out of love for my daughter, or do I truly belong to you?"

All through that beautiful service I prayed and prayed and prayed.

Then, suddenly, I saw Master standing in front of me. His arms were outstretched the way I have often stood before my children, calling them to me. Later I saw a painting of Master, standing on a hill, in just the way I saw him.

"Oh, Mama!" my daughter said when I told her, "Do you know how special your experience was?"

I knew it was special, but I didn't know it was unusual. I thought Master came to welcome everyone. Soon after, I moved to Ananda.

—from Anonymous

Peace At Last

My coworker and I were both sincere in our desire to serve God, but so different in the way we understood just about everything else that conflict was inevitable. For me, kindness is a primary value. I strive for excellence in what I do, but above all I want people to feel respected and included. Perhaps I go too much with people's likes and dislikes when I should hold more strongly to principles.

Whatever tendency I had in that direction was more than compensated for by this man's zealous commitment to doing things "right," as he defined it.

Still, I was surprised by the intensity of his campaign against me. He never seemed to pass up a chance to belittle me or criticize my work. His negativity played right into my insecurity. Perhaps even worse for me, I was not his only target.

My heart is *too* tender. Even when others were able to shrug off what he said against them, *I* felt wounded for *their* sakes. Working with him became a torment and we had to work together almost every day.

I appealed to Swami Kriyananda for help. He was sympathetic, but his only comment was, "As you become stronger the tests become harder, until you become one with God. How else will you evolve spiritually except by being tested in the cold light of day?"

Things went on this way for ten long years. Sometimes I tried to talk to my coworker about the effect he had on me and others, but he was either oblivious or unconcerned.

I meditated often on Swamiji's words. That didn't resolve the situation, but it did help to make it less personal. I thanked God for trusting me enough to give me such a hard test.

Finally I made a firm resolution. Some part of me, I realized, was waiting for *him* to change. In deep meditation I prayed harder than I ever had before. "Dear Lord, what can I do to resolve this situation?"

The conflict at the time centered around a project which I wanted to carry forward and he was determined to thwart. After a time of heartfelt prayer, I surrendered all attachment to the project that had meant so much to me just a moment before.

As I surrendered, I felt the grace of God envelop me like a warm embrace. I looked into my heart and found nothing there but kindness toward my coworker. Years of frustration simply disappeared, dissolved by the grace of God.

Later that day when I saw him, I was completely relaxed and my heart was open—instead of braced as I usually was, anticipating the next blow. His voice, which had begun to grate on my nerves, now sounded sweet.

Even more amazing, his feelings toward me also changed. The test was over. From one day to the next we went from being antagonists to friends.

Before this, I had understood that God's grace was all-powerful. Now I had *experienced* it.

I wrote to Swamiji about the miraculous change. Usually he would answer my letters with one of his own. This time, even though he was out of the country, he telephoned.

"I am so proud of you," he said.

—from Anonymous

ACROSS *the* WATER

My daughter was six when Ron married us. We had twelve wonderful years together. Then, at the age of forty-seven, Ron died of cancer.

The cancer had surfaced four years earlier. But, after surgery, he was declared "cancer free" and sent home without further treatment. He was still in a lot of pain; but when his doctors recommended nothing more than codeine pills, we accepted their decision without question.

In retrospect it seems obvious we were scared and didn't want to know what else might be going on inside his body. Three years passed in relatively good health. Then Ron expressed a desire to visit the Holy Land.

We had explored the spiritual path together, reading *Autobiography of a Yogi,* among other books. I was immediately drawn to Yogananda, and later to Ananda; Ron was lukewarm about it, but supported me in my interest.

It was the summer of 1984. Our daughter was eighteen, and the trip seemed ideal for all of us. On the strength of my job as a schoolteacher, I was able to borrow $10,000 to cover the cost. We had a fabulous journey together—our last, as it turned out. Again, in retrospect, some part of me knew what would take place; that's why I didn't think twice about going into debt to make that trip happen.

A few months later, Ron developed what appeared to be a terrible flu. He could hardly eat and had to be hospitalized. Tests soon revealed that the cancer had metastasized. My formerly big, strong husband left the hospital in a wheelchair and was never able to walk again. From then on he needed constant care.

Most of the time I took care of Ron myself. Only when his mother came from Ohio to our home in California to be with him did I feel comfortable leaving. I would go to Ananda Village, to rest and to pray for Ron.

In early July 1985, Ron was very ill in the hospital. His mother was there, and I was assured it would be fine for me to go. Ron was fully conscious when I said good-bye to him, never imagining it was good-bye for the last time.

At Ananda, one of the ministers invited me to take formal initiation as a disciple of Paramhansa Yogananda. By that time I had learned to meditate and was regularly practicing the teachings, but it hadn't occurred to me to take initiation. I wasn't entirely sure what it meant, but some deeper part of me understood. "Yes," I said.

I was initiated on Sunday morning, July 7. Afterwards, as I was kneeling in front of Master's picture, I had a vision of my husband and me sitting together in a small rowboat. He was in the front; I was working the oars, moving the boat forward. He was as I had last seen him, too sick and debilitated to help me row.

Master appeared, walked across the water, and stood silently in front of the boat. My husband, who hadn't walked in months, stood up easily, got out of the boat and joined him. On the horizon, toward the left,

Light appeared. I watched as Ron and Master walked over the water and into the Light.

A beautiful, bright blue, female figure appeared in front of me. "Who are you?" I asked.

"Divine Mother," she answered.

Later that day I found out Ron had died. At first I felt terrible guilt that I wasn't with him when he passed. Gradually though, I came to understand that God had taken me to Ananda to give me initiation.

If I had been sitting with Ron in the hospital room, I believe my attachment to him, and his to me, would have made the transition difficult. This way, my love for God, my love for Ron, and my commitment as a disciple opened the way for Master to come and take my beloved husband into the Light.

Knowing how devastated I would be, I believe Divine Mother came also, to remind me that even though the form of love changes, the death of a loved one is not the end of love.

—from Sheila Nichols

OUR LADY

After three weeks in the meditative quiet of the Ananda Retreat near Assisi, Italy, it was a shock to be back in the "real world." The coarse laughter of the young men standing near me in the train station grated on my now finely tuned nervous system. The train to Rome was just the first stage of almost two days of travel to get back home to Finland. I speak English, but hardly a word of Italian, and I rarely travel alone. I felt isolated and a little afraid.

I comforted myself by listening to Swami Kriyananda chanting AUM through my MP3 player. The chant was suddenly interrupted by a crude grinding sound as the player stopped working.

I tried to visualize Master standing next to me as my "bodyguard." Then I thought, "Divine Mother *is* the AUM always surrounding me." I prayed to Her, "Divine Mother, be with me not only in Spirit, but also in a way that I can feel physically, so that I won't be afraid."

At that very instant a large group of English-speaking people came into the station, many wearing badges with a picture of the Virgin Mary. "That was quick," I said to Divine Mother.

They were pilgrims just returning from Medjugorje in Croatia, where the Virgin Mary has appeared many times to a small group of visionaries. The pilgrims must have recognized me as a kindred spirit, because immediately I became part of their group. They offered to help with my luggage, and we all boarded the train together. It turned out my seat was right in the middle of their section. The group leader, a sweet middle-aged woman, was sitting next to me. All the way to Rome we talked happily about God and Divine Mother—the Virgin Mary to them, but we all agreed we loved the same Lady in different forms.

Just before we got to Rome, the group leader said to me, "Our Lady has asked me to give you something." She handed me her personal rosary. "It is hard for me to give this away," she admitted. "I have had it a long time, and have prayed with it in many sacred places. But Our Lady is urging me now to give it to you, to protect you on your journey, and I always do what She asks."

It was only then that I told her, my eyes filled with grateful tears, that just before her group had arrived, I was feeling afraid and had prayed to Divine Mother to take care of me.

—from Tyagini Naima

Let There Be Light

No one in my family understood the urgency of my spiritual quest and why it led me to meditation and discipleship to an Indian guru. We were third generation South Dakota farmers. If you felt religious you could choose from a variety of Christian churches right there in town. My choice was, to them, incomprehensible.

My husband felt especially threatened by what I was doing. He was one of ten children in a family that had been financially ruined by the Great Depression. He grew up on welfare and vowed that when he became a husband and father, he would *always* be able to provide for his family. He made good on his vow and cared not only for me and our children, but my extended family and his as well. A person with his background might easily have become miserly. Instead, he became compassionate and generous to others in need.

When I began to meditate, and became devoted to Paramhansa Yogananda as my guru, my husband felt I was shutting him out. Someone had become more important to me than he and the family we had created together. I tried every way I could to show him that loving God and

Guru didn't mean I loved our family less. Love is infinite, not finite as he thought it to be.

But in a sense, his intuition was correct. Much as I loved my family and was grateful to my husband for a lifetime of hard work and loving care, nothing was more important to me than my relationship with God and Guru.

He never got over what he saw as my betrayal of him. Not long after I got on the spiritual path, he was stricken with cancer.

Despite his disapproval, I was determined to carry on with my spiritual practices. I couldn't let meditation interfere with my care for him and my family. That would have brought even more criticism down upon my head.

Early in the morning was the obvious time to meditate. My husband woke every day to an alarm set for 7:15 a.m. We slept in the same room and if I set an earlier alarm, it would wake him too, and that was obviously a bad idea.

One night I prayed urgently, "I have been a spiritual seeker all my life. Now that I have found this path and this practice, I *must* find a way to carry on with it. Please help me to wake up early."

At 6:00 a.m. the next morning I was sound asleep when the lamp on my bedside table suddenly turned on, shining directly into my face. I woke immediately, turned off the light, and got up to meditate for a full hour. Then I slipped back into bed and was lying there quietly content when the alarm went off as usual at 7:15.

Every morning after that, whenever my husband and I slept in that room, the light went on at exactly 6:00 a.m.

Five years later my husband died, still adamantly opposed to my spiritual life. Many times in my meditation after he passed I tried to contact his soul. I would talk to him, explaining again in words I hoped he could now understand, why loving God made it possible for me to love him *more*, not less.

A few months after he died, I had a vivid, superconscious dream about him. Yogananda was also there, and when I tried to introduce my husband to my Guru, he looked sternly at Yogananda and said firmly, "Don't say a word or there will be a fight!" Despite death and all my efforts to explain, he remained fixed in his point of view.

Silently, with great love, Yogananda looked deep into his eyes. My husband, too, simply stared back without saying a word. Then, to my astonishment and delight, my husband turned to me and melted into my arms. Finally, I felt, he understood.

The division between us dissolved. In this shared understanding of Yogananda's love, I felt closer to my husband in death than I ever did when he was alive.

I feel that death itself was his last generous act to me. On some level I believe he chose to die to free me to follow my spiritual path. Even though my children still disapproved, after his passing I left South Dakota and came to live on the West Coast where I could be part of an Ananda community. That would have been impossible if my husband had still been alive.

—from Lajjana

WHITE BIRD

I was on my third coast-to-coast bicycle trip—this time starting in California, and ending in Virginia. We began as a rather disjointed group of seven. No one person was familiar with more than one or two of the others. Without friendship to unite us, we soon separated according to how fast we liked to ride.

My partner was a man with whom I shared nothing except our pace. Soon that tenuous bond broke, and most days I was alone, which suited me fine. There is safety in numbers, but even on group rides I usually found a way to spend most of the time by myself.

This day it was pouring rain and by mid-afternoon already dark. I had been riding for hours with my head down, watching nothing but the spinning tire and the wet road in front of me. Slick pavement is dangerous, and to make matters worse, there was construction going on and sometimes debris on the road.

I had no idea where my companion was. Miles ahead or miles behind, I didn't know. Suddenly it occurred to me that I was completely alone, in dangerous conditions, in a part of the country known to be hostile to cyclists. In this area, they don't appreciate our fancy bikes and funny clothes. Sometimes they express their displeasure by throwing beer cans and bottles at us as they whiz by in their cars.

Most of the time riding my bike, I feel a wonderful sense of freedom and self-reliance. Nothing holds me back; I can go anywhere, do anything. Now I felt a sudden anxiety. After hours of riding in the cold, wet weather, my hands and feet were numb, which would make it harder to get away if I had to flee.

The Jesuits say, "Give us a child until the age of ten and we'll have him for life." There must be some truth in this, because in my hour of need what I drew upon was the training I had received as a child from my devout Catholic mother.

She was fond of calling upon God. "Offer Thee, Sweet Jesus," my mother would say. Or, when in need of help, "Come, Holy Ghost."

Alone on my bicycle, I found myself chanting, "Come, Holy Ghost. Come, Holy Ghost. Come, Holy Ghost." A few minutes later something white by the side of the road caught my attention. I hadn't looked up all day. Now I glanced to the left.

Spray-painted on a big granite rock were the words "HOLY GHOST."

"Thanks!" I said to God, the Holy Ghost, and my long-departed Catholic mother. Anxiety vanished, and I relaxed again into the pure joy of cycling.

When the ride was over, I decided to visit my sister in New Jersey before heading back to California. I could have cycled to her place, but once I reached the Atlantic Ocean, I was ready for a break. I put myself and my bike on a bus heading north.

I found two empty seats together and settled down by the window for a quiet, comfortable ride. Just before the doors closed, a big, tough-looking guy got on. The only seat left on the bus was the one next to me. Instead of two seats, now I had three-quarters of one.

Looks are deceiving. He turned out to be a real sweetheart. We had a delightful conversation all the way to his stop a few towns before mine. "I feel we are just becoming friends, and now you have to go," I said sadly.

He reached into his pocket and pulled out a tiny figurine of a sparkling white bird. "The bird of friendship," he said as he handed it to me.

Every good Catholic girl knows what the white dove represents. "Come, Holy Ghost," I had said, and there It was in the center of my palm.

—from Rita Deierlein

DESERT HIKE

I am only half-joking when I say that, before I incarnated on Earth, I spent most of my lifetimes on a planet closer to the Sun. My enthusiasm for hot, dry weather borders on the extreme. Fortunately my wife enjoys the desert almost as much as I do.

We had been to Palm Desert before and our routine was pretty well worked out: lots of time hiking outdoors. Usually I'm strong from day one, and it takes my wife a little while to adapt. So it was surprising the first morning that she was full of energy while I was dragging myself along.

Still, we set out as planned on a twelve-mile hike to an oasis and back. It was hot, probably peaking at 112 degrees, but we were dressed for it and carried plenty of food and water.

One of the things I enjoy about hiking is that it gives me hours and hours to chant, mentally or out loud. "O God Beautiful" is one of my favorite hiking songs. I also often repeat the mantra, "AUM Babaji." Babaji is the Himalayan yogi in our line of gurus, and in the wilderness I feel especially close to him.

Halfway to the oasis it was obvious something was very wrong with me. It didn't occur to me to turn back; I assumed I could hike through it. By contrast, my wife was zipping along at the top of her game. At the oasis we rested and ate lunch. If I could have teleported myself back to the car, I would have. There was no choice, however, except to walk the six miles out the way we had come in.

I'm not one to complain, so we didn't talk about it. I just said I needed to go slow. She took the lead and stayed about twenty-five yards in front of me; stopping every so often to make sure I was still following; calling my name occasionally; pausing when I had to pause. Even though I hadn't said much, she knew I was in bad shape. I narrowed my focus until I was looking at nothing but her and willed myself to keep walking.

On the way to the oasis I kept "O God Beautiful" going inside my head. On the way back I tried to keep it up, but my energy was sinking fast and the song was more than I could handle. Just repeating "AUM Babaji" was all the concentration I could spare from the effort to keep my feet moving.

Walls seemed to be closing in around me. My band of awareness narrowed and I could feel my life force slipping away. I felt like I was dying. There was even a flock of turkey vultures circling over the trail. Talk about a B-movie script!

But this wasn't a movie. This was serious. I wasn't afraid. I've meditated for years, and I try to live in such a way that when my time comes I can go without regret.

My concern was for my wife. I knew she could live without me; that wasn't the issue. My concern was, "What would she do if I collapsed out here in the desert?" I am a big man; she is a small woman. I didn't think she could even pull my body under a bush, what to speak of lugging me all the way back to the car. I couldn't do that to her.

Every ten steps it seemed I had to stop and rest. And whenever I found a little bit of shade I'd hunker there for a while, then pull myself up and go on.

Through all of this my wife was staying a steady twenty-five yards in front of me. It was good that she was too far away to talk. Anything I said would have scared her and reinforced my feeling of weakness. Having her there kept my mind on where I was going and off my present predicament. I could feel her will power pulling me along behind her. I know for certain that if she hadn't been there, I wouldn't have made it.

After about three miles my life review started. Long-forgotten events of my childhood started happening all around me. Not only images, but also sounds: very loud sounds.

Riding my bike on the sidewalk. Swimming in the pool. Eating dinner with my family. Sledding in the winter. Playing basketball with my brothers.

It didn't frighten me that this was happening, but it was *very* distracting, which was the last thing I needed.

AUM Babaji. AUM Babaji. AUM Babaji. Take a few steps. Rest. Drink water. Look at my wife. Start walking again. AUM Babaji. AUM Babaji. AUM Babaji. All the while my childhood was repeating itself in full volume around me.

Although it seemed much longer, it was only six miles, and finally we made it to the plateau just above where the car was parked. A boulder cast a small shadow, so I sat in front of it and leaned back. As soon as I sat down, the life review stopped.

We hadn't seen anyone else the whole time we were out there. Now I looked across the desert, and about thirty feet away I saw a young man sitting perfectly still on a rock ledge in full lotus position, meditating while facing the sun. He was bare-chested and wasn't wearing a hat. His hair was long and reddish colored.

My wife came and sat next to me. She looked over at him and said, "He shouldn't be sitting out in the sun like that with no shirt or hat."

"That's just what I was thinking," I said. "Maybe I should go tell him."

We sat together, watching him sit motionless before us, talking a little about how we hoped he would be okay, exposed to the sun like that. I drank water, splashed water on my face, closed my eyes to rest and opened them again. Always he was there.

After about ten minutes I felt strong enough to go the short distance to the car.

"Before I leave," I thought, "I have to go tell that man to put on a hat."

My wife and I stood up together, and immediately both of us forgot the man was there. We didn't remember we'd seen him until several hours later.

We went to the car, drove home, showered, rehydrated, and were lying on the floor resting in the air-conditioned condo when we remembered him again. This time what had not crossed our minds before was suddenly obvious. Could it have been Babaji? Certainly no ordinary person could have sat utterly still, bare-chested, facing the sun like that. He looked like the pictures of Babaji, and like that great guru he had copper-colored hair.

If I had been alone, given the condition I was in, it would be easy to say I imagined it all. But my wife was there, and she was as clear and energetic at the end of the hike as she had been at the beginning. All the energy that I was lacking seemed to be present in her.

We compared notes and we both had seen exactly the same thing, except for one odd detail: the man had been much closer to me than to her. Was it because I had needed him more? I don't know for sure that I was dying out in the desert that day; but I felt that I was, and I believe Babaji saved me.

—from Anonymous

Two Nurses

My knee was injured in a car accident. The ligaments were torn, and the doctors decided to operate. In the middle of the operation, I left my body. Suddenly all boundaries disappeared. I was as big as the whole room, floating in a sea of luminous light, a delicate shade of golden pink not of this world. Every particle of my being was permeated by a love so great, so pure. I felt I could remain in that state forever. There was no fear or pain, no desire, no body. Just golden pink light and perfect love.

But it did not last. Just as suddenly I was unbearably squeezed, shrunk, and confined to my body again. And now there was pain, and lots of it.

I started shouting, "It's too tight! It's too tight!" I was referring to my body, but the nurse and surgeon thought I meant the plaster cast they were putting on my leg.

"It has to be this tight," the nurse explained, "otherwise you won't heal correctly."

But I was inconsolable and determined to get back to what I had just experienced. Deliberately, I blocked the flow of my breath.

In the operating room, my sudden inability to breathe was seen as a medical emergency. I was rushed to intensive care where an oxygen mask was strapped to my face, forcing air into my lungs.

Two nurses were taking care of me. The one toward the foot of the bed was very busy managing the oxygen machine, the blood pressure pump, and all the other equipment. The second nurse was sitting quietly, just to my right. The mask prevented me from turning my head to get a better look at her. From the corner of my eye, I could see only that she had long brown hair, parted in the center. She adjusted my pillow and stroked my head. Never in my life had I felt so loved.

The battle between my desire to leave my body and the medical effort to keep me in it went on for a long time. Finally, I gave in and began to breathe without being forced to do so by their equipment. My heart and blood pressure stabilized. The medical emergency was over.

The nurse monitoring the equipment removed the mask from my face. My first thought was to thank the nurse next to me for her tender care. I looked to the right, but no one was there.

"Where is the other nurse?" I said to the one working the machines.

"Who?" she asked.

"Your colleague, the one who has been sitting beside me all this time."

"Nobody has been there," she said. "It has just been you and me."

—*from Scilla di Massa*

ROCK *in the*
SNOW FIELD

When we woke at 2:30 a.m., the tent seemed smaller than it had when we crawled in to sleep a few hours earlier. It had begun to snow and the walls were caving in. For the rest of the night, we thumped the nylon periodically to keep the snow from accumulating and collapsing the tent. We were sleepless, but not too worried. Wilderness backpacking is something my wife Maghi and I have been doing for years.

We were camped by a lake 10,500 feet up in the Wind River Mountains of Wyoming, miles from everywhere. It had taken three days of hard walking to get there, through some steep rockslides with boulders as big as houses. Rain and sleet on the way up had made hiking difficult, snow would make going down that way impossible. It was too early for snow, but the storm hadn't read the almanac.

Our plan was to make a loop—to stay one night at this lake then hike over the pass another thousand feet above us. The way up from here was a poorly marked switchback trail, impossible to discern now in the snow.

To make things worse, both of us had come down with sinus infections. We had a good medical kit and started right in with antibiotics. Still, we spent a miserable three nights and two days in the tent in the snow, trying to find in our trail mix and freeze-dried foods something that wasn't too hard for our inflamed throats to swallow.

I spent a lot of time looking through binoculars at the route to the pass, hoping to find enough landmarks to take us safely across. There wasn't much to see. Snow makes everything really quiet, and in three days, camped right by the trail, we neither saw nor heard another human being.

We were praying a lot to Babaji, the ever-living Himalayan yogi, figuring he was the one who could help us out of this jam. Finally there was a small break in the weather. Snow still covered the switchback trail, but we knew we had to get out of there and the pass was the only way.

Shortly after we started walking, we saw booted footprints on the trail going just the direction we wanted to go. Everybody these days, going through such rough terrain, uses hiking poles. But there was no sign of poles, just footprints. They continued all the way up the switchback, which would have been impossible to find without the prints to guide us. At one point they led us off the main trail to a little lake, then they came back again and continued up toward the pass.

About halfway to the top we stopped to rest against a large rock. Close to the ground there was an overhang sheltering a small grassy area untouched by snow. Maghi leaned over and underneath saw what looked like a little grass-carpeted natural chapel, complete with a discolored marking on the back "wall" in the shape of an arch, just the right size for a wallet-size picture of Babaji. We imagined him sitting there in his tiny rock chapel and prayed for his blessing.

We reached the pass and started down the other side. The snow was a little thinner here, and not too far ahead we could see the trail down. At that point the footprints turned to the right. We weren't depending on them now, and they were going where we didn't want to go, but of course, we followed, hoping to catch up with our mysterious benefactor.

The footprints led to a large boulder in the middle of a smooth, snow-covered field. There they stopped.

—from Vasanta

ABOUT *the* AUTHOR

Asha Praver is a lifelong disciple of the great spiritual master and world teacher, Paramhansa Yogananda (author of the classic *Autobiography of a Yogi*), and has studied for

 more than forty years with Yogananda's close and direct disciple, Swami Kriyananda. Asha has devoted her life to bringing spiritual understanding to others through teaching, counseling, and writing. Toward that end her lectures in the United States and around the world, and letters to spiritual seekers and other writings, are made available through her website: **nayaswamiasha.org**. Along with her husband David, Asha is co-director of the spiritual work and community known as Ananda Palo Alto. She is also the author of *Swami Kriyananda: As We Have Known Him.*

with CRYSTAL CLARITY

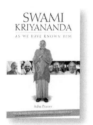

Swami Kriyananda
AS WE HAVE KNOWN HIM
Asha Praver

The greatness of a spiritual teacher is only partially revealed by the work of his own hands. The rest of the story is one he cannot tell for himself. It is the influence of his consciousness on those who come in contact with him—whether for a brief moment, or for a lifetime of spiritual training. This is the story told here.

Swami Kriyananda, a foremost disciple of Paramhansa Yogananda (author of *Autobiography of a Yogi*) has been prodigiously creative in his service to his Guru. His books are available in 28 languages in 100 countries. His music is performed around the world. In India, millions of people watch his daily television show. He has founded schools and retreats, and communities on three continents. He speaks eight languages, and has circled the globe dozens of times lecturing and teaching.

In this "biography of consciousness," Swami Kriyananda's remarkable qualities are revealed with breathtaking clarity—love for God, divinely guided strength, joy in the face of adversity, humor, wisdom, compassion, and unconditional love. Here, in some two hundred stories spanning more than forty years, personal reminiscences and private moments with this beloved teacher become universal life lessons for us all.

The original 1946 unedited edition of Yogananda's spiritual masterpiece

Autobiography of a Yogi

Paramhansa Yogananda

Autobiography of a Yogi is one of the best-selling Eastern philosophy titles of all time, with millions of copies sold, named one of the best and most influential books of the twentieth century. This highly prized reprinting of the original 1946 edition is the only one available free from textual changes made after Yogananda's death. Yogananda was the first yoga master of India whose mission was to live and teach in the West.

In this updated edition are bonus materials, including a last chapter that Yogananda wrote in 1951, without posthumous changes. This new edition also includes the eulogy that Yogananda wrote for Gandhi, and a new fore-word and afterword by Swami Kriyananda.

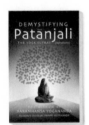

Demystifying Patanjali

The Yoga Sutras (Aphorisms)
The Wisdom of Paramhansa Yogananda, by Swami Kriyananda

What happens as we grow spiritually? Is there a step-by-step process that everyone goes through—all spiritual seekers—as they gradually work their way upward, until they achieve the highest state of Self-realization? About 2200 years ago, a great spiritual master of India named Patanjali presented humanity with a clear-cut, step-by-step outline of how all truth seekers and saints achieve divine union. He called this univer-sal inner experience and process "yoga" or "union." His collection of profound aphorisms—a true world scripture—has been dubbed Patanjali's Yoga Sutras.

Now, a modern yoga master—Paramhansa Yogananda—has resurrected Patan-jali's original revelations. Swami Kriyananda shares Yogananda's crystal clear and easy-to-grasp explanations of Patanjali's aphorisms.

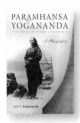

Paramhansa Yogananda

A Biography with Personal Reflections
and Reminiscences *by Swami Kriyananda*

Paramhansa Yogananda's classic *Autobiography of a Yogi* is more about the saints Yogananda met than about himself—in spite of Yogananda's astonishing accomplishments.

Now, one of Yogananda's direct disciples relates the untold story of this great spiritual master and world teacher: his teenage miracles, his challenges in coming to America, his national lecture campaigns, his struggles to fulfill his world-changing mission amid incomprehension and painful betrayals, and his ultimate triumphant achievement. Kriyananda's subtle grasp of his guru's inner nature reveals Yogananda's many-sided greatness. Includes many never-before-published anecdotes.

The New Path

My Life with Paramhansa Yogananda
Swami Kriyananda

Winner of the 2010 Eric Hoffer Award for Best Self-Help/Spiritual Book
Winner of the 2010 USA Book News Award for Best Spiritual Book

This is the moving story of Kriyananda's years with Paramhansa Yogananda, India's emissary to the West and the first yoga master to spend the greater part of his life in America. When Swami Kriyananda discovered *Autobiography of a Yogi* in 1948, he was totally new to Eastern teachings. This is a great advantage to the Western reader, since Kriyananda walks us along the yogic path as he discovers it from the moment of his initiation as a disciple of Yogananda. With winning honesty, humor, and deep insight, he shares his exciting journey along the spiritual path.

Through more than four hundred stories of life with Yogananda, we tune in more deeply to this great master and to the teachings he brought to the West. This book is an ideal complement to *Autobiography of a Yogi*.

The Essence of the Bhagavad Gita

Explained by Paramhansa Yogananda
As Remembered by his disciple, Swami Kriyananda

Rarely in a lifetime does a new spiritual classic appear that has the power to change people's lives and transform future generations. This is such a book.

This revelation of India's best-loved scripture approaches it from a fresh perspective, showing its deep allegorical meaning and its down-to-earth practicality. The themes presented are universal: how to achieve victory in life in union with the divine; how to prepare for life's "final exam," death, and what happens afterward; and how to triumph over all pain and suffering.

"It is doubtful that there has been a more important spiritual writing in the last fifty years .... What a gift! What a treasure!" —**Neale Donald Walsch**, author of *Conversations with God*

Revelations of Christ

Proclaimed by Paramhansa Yogananda
Presented by his disciple, Swami Kriyananda

The rising tide of alternative beliefs proves that now, more than ever, people are yearning for a clear-minded and uplifting understanding of the life and teachings of Jesus Christ.

This galvanizing book, presenting the teachings of Christ from the experience and perspective of Paramhansa Yogananda, one of the greatest spiritual masters of the twentieth century, finally offers the fresh perspective on Christ's teachings for which the world has been waiting. This work gives us an opportunity to understand and apply the scriptures in a more reliable way than any other: by studying under those saints who have communed directly, in deep ecstasy, with Christ and God.

"Kriyananda's revelatory book gives us the enlightened, timeless wisdom of Jesus the Christ in a way that addresses the challenges of twenty-first-century living."

—**Michael Beckwith**, Founder and Spiritual Director, Agape International Spiritual Center, author of *Inspirations of the Heart*

Conversations with Yogananda

Recorded, Compiled, and Edited with commentary by his disciple, Swami Kriyananda

Here is an unparalleled, firsthand account of the teachings of Paramhansa Yogananda. Featuring nearly 500 never-before-released stories, sayings, and insights, this is an extensive, yet eminently accessible treasure trove of wisdom from one of the 20th century's most famous yoga masters. Compiled and edited with commentary by Swami Kriyananda, one of Yogananda's closest direct disciples.

The Essence of Self-Realization

The Wisdom of Paramhansa Yogananda
Recorded, Compiled, and Edited by his disciple, Swami Kriyananda

With nearly three hundred sayings rich with spiritual wisdom, this book is the fruit of a labaor of love. A glance at the table of contents will convince the reader of the vast scope of this work. It offers as complete an explanation of life's true purpose, and of the way to achieve that purpose, as may be found anywhere.

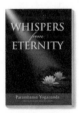

Whispers from Eternity

Paramhansa Yogananda
Edited by his disciple, Swami Kriyananda

Many poetic works can inspire, but few, like this one, have the power to change your life. Yogananda was not only a spiritual master, but a master poet, whose verses revealed the hidden divine presence behind even everyday things. This book has the power to rapidly accelerate your spiritual growth, and provides hundreds of delightful ways for you to begin your own conversation with God.

"This is one of my all-time favorite books"—**Krysta Gibson,** *New Spirit Journal*

THE WISDOM *of* YOGANANDA SERIES

This series features writings of Paramhansa Yogananda not available elsewhere—including many from his earliest years in America—in an approachable, easy-to-read format. The words of the Master are presented with minimal editing, to capture his expansive and compassionate wisdom, his sense of fun, and his practical guidance.

How to Be Happy All the Time
The Wisdom of Yogananda Series, VOLUME 1

Yogananda powerfully explains virtually everything needed to lead a happier, more fulfilling life. Topics include: looking for happiness in the right places; choosing to be happy; tools and techniques for achieving happiness; sharing happiness with others; balancing success and happiness; and many more.

Karma and Reincarnation
The Wisdom of Yogananda Series, VOLUME 2

Yogananda reveals the truth behind karma, death, reincarnation, and the afterlife. With clarity and simplicity, he makes the mysterious understandable. Topics include: why we see a world of suffering and inequality; how to handle the challenges in our lives; what happens at death, and after death; and the purpose of reincarnation.

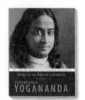

Spiritual Relationships
The Wisdom of Yogananda Series, VOLUME 3

This book contains practical guidance and fresh insight on relationships of all types, including: how to cure bad habits that can end true friendship; how to choose the right partner; how to conceive a spiritual child; and the Universal Love behind all relationships.

How to Be a Success

The Wisdom of Yogananda Series, VOLUME 4

This book includes the complete text of *The Attributes of Success*, the original booklet later published as *The Law of Success*. In addition, you will learn how to find your purpose in life, develop habits of success and eradicate habits of failure, develop your will power and magnetism, and thrive in the right job.

How to Have Courage, Calmness, and Confidence

The Wisdom of Yogananda Series, VOLUME 5

Winner 2011 International Book Award: Best Self-Help Title

This book shows you how to transform your life. Dislodge negative thoughts and depression. Uproot fear and thoughts of failure. Cure nervousness and eliminate worry from your life. Overcome anger, sorrow, oversensitivity, and a host of other troublesome emotional responses; and much more.

How to Achieve Glowing Health and Vitality

The Wisdom of Yogananda Series, VOLUME 6

Paramhansa Yogananda offers practical, wide-ranging, and fascinating suggestions on how to have more energy and live a radiantly healthy life. The principles in this book promote physical health and all-round well-being, mental clarity, and ease and inspiration in your spiritual life.

Readers will discover the priceless Energization Exercises for rejuvenating the body and mind, the fine art of conscious relaxation, and helpful diet tips for health and beauty.

Self-Expansion Through Marriage
A Way to Inner Happiness
Swami Kriyananda

Marriage, understood and lived expansively, is a path to transcendent love—to realization of one's higher spiritual potential. This practical and inspiring guide will help you follow the deeper call of your relationship, enriching not only your marriage, but your life.

Meditation for Starters
Swami Kriyananda

Have you wanted to learn to meditate, but just never got around to it? Or tried "sitting in the silence" only to find yourself too restless to stay more than a few moments? If so, *Meditation for Starters* is just what you've been looking for—and with a companion CD, it provides everything you need to begin a meditation practice.

Filled with easy-to-follow instructions, beautiful guided visualizations, and answers to important questions on meditation, the book includes: what meditation is (and isn't); how to relax your body and prepare yourself for going within; and techniques for interiorizing and focusing the mind.

Awaken to Superconsciousness
Swami Kriyananda

This popular guide includes everything you need to know about the philosophy and practice of meditation, and how to apply the meditative mind to resolve common daily conflicts in uncommon, superconscious ways.

Superconsciousness is the hidden mechanism at work behind intuition, spiritual and physical healing, successful problem solving, and finding deep and lasting joy.

Living Wisely, Living Well

Swami Kriyananda

**Winner 2011 International Book Award:
Best Self-Help Motivational Title**

Want to transform your life? Get inspired, uplifted, and motivated? Here are 366 practical ways to improve your life—a thought for each day of the year. Each reading is warm with wisdom, alive with positive expectation, and provides simple actions that bring profound results.

The Rubaiyat of Omar Khayyam Explained

Paramhansa Yogananda, edited by Swami Kriyananda

The *Rubaiyat* is loved by Westerners as a hymn of praise to sensual delights. In the East its quatrains are considered a deep allegory of the soul's romance with God, based solely on the author Omar Khayyam's reputation as a sage and mystic. But for centuries the meaning of this famous poem has remained a mystery. Now Paramhansa Yogananda reveals the secret import and the "golden spiritual treasures" hidden behind the *Rubaiyat*'s verses—and presents a new scripture to the world.

Education for Life

According to Paramhansa Yogananda Edited by Swami Kriyananda

A constructive and brilliant alternative to what has been called the disaster of modern education; the statistics of illiteracy, drug abuse, and violence speak for themselves. In this book, Kriyananda traces the problems to an emphasis on technological competence at the expense of spiritual values, which alone can give higher meaning to life. *Education for Life* offers parents, educators, and concerned citizens everywhere techniques that are both compassionate and practical.

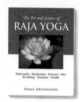

The Art and Science of Raja Yoga
Swami Kriyananda

This book contains fourteen lessons in which the original yoga science emerges in all its glory—a proven system for realizing one's spiritual destiny. This is the most comprehensive course available on yoga and meditation today. Over 450 pages of text and photos give you a complete and detailed presentation of yoga postures, yoga philosophy, affirmations, meditation instruction, and breathing practices.

Also included are suggestions for daily yoga routines, information on proper diet, recipes, and alternative healing techniques.

The Art of Supportive Leadership
A Practical Guide for People in Positions of Responsibility
J. Donald Walters (Swami Kriyananda)

You can learn to be a more effective leader by viewing leadership in terms of shared accomplishments rather than personal advancement. Drawn from timeless Eastern wisdom, this book is clear, concise, and practical—designed to produce results quickly and simply. Used in training seminars in the U.S., Europe, and India, this book helps increase effectiveness, creativity, and team building in companies everywhere.

Money Magnetism
How to Attract What You Need When You Need It
J. Donald Walters (Swami Kriyananda)

This book can change your life by transforming how you think and feel about money. According to the author, anyone can attract wealth: "There need be no limits to the flow of your abundance." With true stories and examples, Swami Kriyananda vividly—sometimes humorously—shows you how the principles of money magnetism work, and how you can start applying them today to achieve greater success in your material and your spiritual life.

How to Meditate
A Step-by-Step Guide to the Art & Science of Meditation
Jyotish Novak

This clear and concise guidebook contains everything you need to start your practice. With easy-to-follow instructions, meditation teacher Jyotish Novak demystifies meditation—presenting the essential techniques so that you can quickly grasp them. Since it was first published in 1989, *How to Meditate* has helped thousands to establish a regular meditation routine. This newly revised edition includes a bonus chapter on scientific studies showing the benefits of meditation, plus all-new photographs and illustrations.

The Time Tunnel
A Tale for All Ages and for the Child in You
Swami Kriyananda

This story explores life-enhancing spiritual truths through the eyes of two young boys, including how to find true happiness, what qualities bring unhappiness, how positive expectations bring positive results, and what values are important. Richly imaginative and inventive, *The Time Tunnel* conveys deep truths in a way that will provide adults and children with fascinating topics for discussion..

Please visit our website to view all our available titles in books, as well as other products—audiobooks, spoken word, music, and DVDs.

WWW.CRYSTALCLARITY.COM

CRYSTAL CLARITY PUBLICATIONS

Crystal Clarity Publishers offers additional resources to assist you in your spiritual journey, including many other books, a wide variety of inspirational and relaxation music composed by Swami Kriyananda, and yoga and meditation videos.

Crystal Clarity Publishers / www.crystalclarity.com
14618 Tyler Foote Rd. / Nevada City, CA 95959
TOLL FREE: 800.424.1055 or 530.478.7600 / FAX: 530.478.7610
EMAIL: clarity@crystalclarity.com

ANANDA WORLDWIDE

Ananda Sangha, a worldwide organization founded by Swami Kriyananda, offers spiritual support and resources based on the teachings of Paramhansa Yogananda. There are Ananda spiritual communities in Nevada City, Sacramento, Palo Alto, and Los Angeles, California; Seattle, Washington; Portland and Laurelwood, Oregon; as well as a retreat center and European community in Assisi, Italy, and communities near New Delhi and Pune, India. Ananda supports more than 140 meditation groups worldwide.

For more information about Ananda Sangha, communities, or meditation groups near you, please call 530.478.7560 or visit www.ananda.org.

THE EXPANDING LIGHT

Ananda's guest retreat, The Expanding Light, offers a varied, year-round schedule of classes and workshops on yoga, meditation, and spiritual practice. You may also come for a relaxed personal renewal, participating in ongoing activities as much or as little as you wish. The beautiful serene mountain setting, supportive staff, and delicious vegetarian food provide an ideal environment for a truly meaningful, spiritual vacation.

For more information, please call 800.346.5350 or visit www.expandinglight.org.